Invisible Sides of Insurance Claims

Invisible Sides of Insurance Claims

RP Samal

BLACK EAGLE BOOKS
Dublin, USA | BBSR, India

USA address:
7464 Wisdom Lane
Dublin, OH 43016

India address:
E/312, Trident Galaxy, Kalinga Nagar,
Bhubaneswar-751003, Odisha, India

E-mail: info@blackeaglebooks.org
Website: www.blackeaglebooks.org

First Edition: 2011, Second Edition: 2013

First International Edition Published by
Black Eagle Books, 2024

INVISIBLE SIDES OF INSURANCE CLAIMS
by RP SAMAL

Copyright © RP Samal

All rights reserved. No part of this publication may be reproduced, stored
in a retrieval system, or transmitted, in any form or by any means, electronic,
mechanical, photocopying, recording or otherwise without the prior permission
of the publisher.

Interior Design: Ezy's Publication

ISBN- 978-1-64560-591-1 (Paperback)

Printed in the United States of America

Acknowledgement

Sincerely I express my heartfelt gratitude to Late LP Mehta, Editor of The Asia Insurance Post, to the Editor, The Asia Insurance Review, Singapore and thanks to the Editors of IRDA Journal, Pravartak, the official journal of National Insurnace Acadamy,Pune, The Pioneer, New Delhi for having published some of the chapters of this book. I express my sincere thanks to my friend Prof. M.Simanchal Rao who used his profound scholarly wisdom to discipline the language to convey exactly the way I intended to convey.I am thankful to Shri. K.K.Panda Ex-DGM United India Insurance,CA Sanjeeb Kumar Mohanty and Gayatri Iyer of NIA for sharing some of their valuable experiences. Many thanks to Heena who in her angelic gesture extended all the help in completing this book. Finally I am prayerful to the Almighty without whose grace neither thoughts come nor words speak effectively.

Author

Opinions that Inspires Confidence

This Book is held by connoisseurs of the insurance world as a panacea that would cure the PSU General Insurance Industry bleeding with gargantuan losses.

The Pioneer

The creation of a world class insurance industry presupposes world class thinkers. Here is an attempt by R.P.Samal to protect the industry of today to become world class tomorrow.

Dr.K.C.Mishra, *Ex-Vice Chanceller,*
Sri Sri University ,Cuttack,Odisha

This book is a brilliant attempt in highlighting the importance of effective claims management. The author has marshaled his vast experience in the industry and given valuable tips and advices to claims managers in a lucid and practical way. There are large number of case studies with emphasis on steps to be taken to manage claims efficiently. The book would be an asset for the claims managers in their day to day handling of claims.

G. Srinivasan, Ex-CMD
The New India Assurance Co.Ltd

The book provides cutting edge tips to claim managers which will transform their sight into insight and intelligence into intuition.

NSR Chandraprasad, Ex-CMD
The National Insurance Co.Ltd

What is inside

CHAPTER 1

*Genius is one percent inspiration and
99 percent perspiration.*

Claims and Extraordinary Settlements

Two years after the death of her husband, the widow discovered that her late husband had a personal accident policy for Rs 1lakh. Immediately she intimated the concerned insurance company and completed the necessary formalities. Ten months after her tireless followup she got a no-claim letter which read that two years delay in intimating the company was too long a time to entertain the claim. Out of utter despair and helplessness she wrote to the CMD of the company stating pathetically but with an emphatic note that this was her rightful money and she should not be deprived of it. The tone of her letter had the convincing proof of her honesty. With his mind filled with pragmatism, the CMD had a different pattern of understanding. After going through the details, he reasoned with the concerned regional manager stating that if his office could take ten months in deciding to make it no-claim, which they could have done immediately, what was wrong on the part of the widow to take two years when the delay was beyond her control? The regional manager was speechless and the claim was paid immediately. While receiving the claim cheque, tears welled up in the eyes of the widow. A flicker of new aliveness dawned upon the otherwise dull routine of the company's daily work. A throb of divinity was felt for a while. Such unnoticed details of good deeds needed to be brought to the notice of the world to inspire more such good deeds.

Simplifying the Procedure

Japanese people are short in height, their poems are short (haiku), their trees are short (bonsai), their MOUs are short but their understanding is great and they live a longer life. The Japanese secrets to longevity are not known but this real life case study may throw some light on the issue. Since the amount exceeded their financial limit, a motor total loss claim file came from the Tokyo office of the underwriters to their head office in Mumbai for settlement containing only four documents: driving license proof, original policy, registration certificate, one photograph of the damaged vehicle taken by the concerned branch manager revealing the precarious condition of the vehicle and one line recommendation stating that our branch manager had inspected the vehicle at the site of accident. and he was more than satisfied that the vehicle was a total loss. No survey report and no mile-long estimate of repair. The technical department was satisfied and the claim approval was sent.

Why cannot we be more like that? When it is obvious that the vehicle has been crushed to mangled rubbles, what is the necessity of following a slew of procedures like getting an elaborate estimate which is nothing but the sum total of all parts a new car is made of and obtaining a survey report running into pages which again costs a lot of money and also reading those dry details takes away our precious time of life.That is why the most famous Commerce Bank has its "kill the stupid rule"program whereby employees get $100 when they identify a rule that interferes with giving customers wow experience. Only a technician needs so many documents but a true manager asks for the vital and relevant few.

The Little good Deed

'Great opportunity to help others seldom comes but small ones surround us daily'. For example it was in the year 2007 a middle aged widow met the Chief

Manager of New India Assurance in Mumbai with bruised sentiments that her doctor husband, a master of surgery, had died in a road accident in 2002 and Motor Accident Claim Tribunal had awarded an amount of Rs. 19 lakh (13 lakh + 6 lakh interest) towards compensation. The divisional manager had decided to go in for appeal against the award because the amount, he thought, was very high, thus denying the victim a well-deserved compensation. This decision had shattered the widow's hopes after five long painful years of waiting for the claim. The sensible Chief Manager contacted the concerned divisional manager who tossed out his argument that the company's dealing advocate had recommended to go in for appeal against the quantum awarded. The chief manager intervened with a mixture of irritation and concern and said since our lawyer himself could not fight it out in MACT, how could he expect it to be fought successfully in the high court? This is sheer waste of money by way of additional interest and expensive fees of high court advocate and there was hardly any case in the history where the amount awarded by MACT had been revised down by the high court.

With conscience playing the lead role, the chief manager could not help feeling a sense of wrongness and advised the DM to deposit the claim amount immediately after completing formalities and it was done. The widow who herself was a doctor of medicine burst into tears of gratitude and for a moment the presence of godliness was being felt in the premises of the office. Every year thousands of such claims are sent for appeal by the casual approach of mindless officers. 'Delay is deadliest form of denial'. The claim managers should have understanding of such sensitive problems by putting themselves in the shoes of the claimant or think for a while the claimant is their brother or sister and decide things. Gandhiji has rightly said, 'there is a higher court than the court of justice and that is the court of conscience. It supersedes all other courts'. Let us be passionate about what we do because 'from what we get, we can make a living but what we give makes a life'. Knowledge of our craft makes us confident and charismatic only when it is used judiciously. This way we shall have a more beautiful and celebrating world of insurance.

Paid when Needed

It is aptly said, 'If something comes to life in others because of you, you have made an approach to immortality'. A paper mill was gutted into ashes. It was financed by a co-operative bank and as usual the insurance was taken by the bank only on the outstanding loan amount as sum insured. Hence it was greatly underinsured. When the claim management team visited, the factory was still burning and the entire family of the insured was wailing bitterly expressing despair. The leader of the claims management team arranged for the site visit of all the officers concerned with the settlement of this claim. Since the factory was insured on reinstatement value basis, the surveyor was asked to make two assessments: one on the basis of market value which was assessed for Rs 76 lakh and the other on the basis of reinstatement which was assessed for Rs 98 lakh. The insured was explained the time consuming and rigorous procedure of taking the claim on re-instatement value basis and the simple procedure of taking it on market value basis and advantages thereof. The insured opted for the latter and the claim was paid exactly 21 days after the occurrence of fire due to non-stop follow-up of tireless officers. He did not have to struggle to re-start his business afresh. He was happy and the underwriters got all the business of the bank back to their account and a letter from the bank with unprecedented admiration for the way the claim was attended to. Such acts negate the criticism that insurance salesman serves up only empty promises and adds carats to the golden moments in insurance history.

Settled with Grace

Twenty odd years back a multi -technology public

sector company placed an order for import of heavy machinery worth Rs 11crore from Japan. The consignment was stowed on the inside edge of the deck. Immediately after leaving the coast of Japan the vessel encountered severe stormy weather and got tossed up and down. In the process the machinery fell from the deck with a thud, made a hole in the hull and allowed forbidden sea water to gush into the ship and create havoc. Although all the crew members were rescued, the ship got split in half and went down to the bottom of the sea thirty nautical miles off Japanese coast. There was heartbreak for the insured because the consignment was not covered. Although the insured's representative in Japan had sent a cable to the underwriters in India asking for coverage, the premium was not paid. They approached the insurance company with their confidence badly shaken. Chances of their getting claim was hanging by a thread. But since for all practical purposes the insured had the sincere intention to insure the consignment, the company's learned board examined the representation of the insured carefully, inspired by the intangible spirit of insurance law, took a very bold decision and approved the claim after completion of formalities thereby making significant departure from the orthodox adherence to the practice of insurance principles. It is almost like underwriting intentions. Thus the weather-beaten insured was brought to the shore of safety. A prudent under writer has beautifully put it,

'Insurance is a business of distress management and the process of claim management is the final moment of truth'.

New India Assurance: Taking insurance to the Space

In 1982, New India Assurance heralded a giant step and created miracle by persuading a reluctant Indian Space Research Organization to insure its satellite Insat 1A. And to everyone's shock and dismay the satellite launching vehicle failed to deliver the satellite in its orbit and was a total loss. The claim amount of US$ 65.5 million came as a divine gift to ISRO in no time, without survey and without much procedural hurdles. Neither history nor anyone in this country has ever cared to talk about this daring adventure of The New India Assurance in restoring fortune at the time of misfortune. But definitely it was a proud moment for insurance industry in India. With this claim amount, it was financially easy for ISRO to send the next satellite without delay. It will forever remain as a testament to the company's willingness to take greater risks.

National Insurance: Touching many a heart with Grace

One act which will touch every human heart and for

which National Insurance Company should feel very proud was the settlement of passengers' liability claims of 23 ONGC engineers for Rs 8.5 lakh each, who died in Mesco airlines helicopter crash while returning in unpredictable monsoon from Mumbai High to Juhu airstrip. Due to the passionate concern of dedicated managers, these claims were settled in a record time of seven days much before the tears had dried up in the eyes of the relatives of the deceased. Such spontaneous act would move any insured into tears of gratitude. Performing duty with such overflowing sense of compassion is a rare phenomenon in the realm of insurance and it needed to have been publicized in a big way but National Insurance maintained a low profile and this gracious act quietly got filed away in oblivion. But certainly it will remain as a perennial source of inspiration for those officers who feel that service to others is the duty best performed. If every claim is attended to with this kind of enthusiasm, it will enhance the beauty of the insurance world.

United India Insurance: Delivering the Best

Claim management is the most exciting trait in the entire transaction of insurance business. Ultimate ecstasy lies in prompt and judicious settlement. Here goes one such glaring example. United India had issued a policy covering offshore assets of ONGC for US$ 13 billion with effect from 11 May 2005. During the cyclonic storm Samundra Surakhsha,the multi-purpose support vessel while approaching the platform, lost control and collided against it causing a major fire on 27 July 2005 at Mumbai High resulting in total damage to its north platform and extensive damage to the ship herself. The claim of such huge sum required dexterous management. In adversity, saying goes, lies the opportunity. The insurance company rose to the occasion and paid a huge sum of Rs 1700 crore and Rs 768.56 crore had been released as on account payment within 50 days from the date of accident. The officers of United India showed a greater understanding of how to handle claims under unfortunate circumstances, showcased their talent in insurance history and demonstrated an ability proving the critics wrong who always complain that insurance companies are high on promise and low on delivery.

Oriental Insurance: Greater attention to smaller Claims

It is a common belief th at high value claims are given all the attention and small claims are made to wait and suffer delay in the meandering bylanes of procedure. But in Oriental the story is different. With launching of service centres for motor own damage claims, the company has created a sort of revolution in claims management. More than 90% of such claims are being settled in eleven days time in some of the centres like Ludhiana and Ghaziabad. Turn Around Time (TAT) is calculated from the date of intimation of the claim to the date of issuance of cheque. As on date the company is having 20 service centres across the country covering around 300 operating offices. The management boasts of centres like Ahmedabad and Chennai which are clearing 96% of tens of thousands of claims in record time of less than two weeks. When you start doing something good, God descends to help you in doing so.

Oriental's Kathmandu office in nineties had the unique way of settling personal accident claims. On receipt of the information of accidental death, the officials used to rush to the family of the insured to get the formalities completed without hurting their sentiments and on the final day of the rituals while offering condolences they used to hand over the claim cheque in the huge gathering of the deceased's kith and kin, a kind of consolation the family needed most. We only need a heart full of grace to do this. How far we go in providing services depends on how quickly we give.

ICICI Lombard: Understanding Responsibility

The effect of any disaster, natural or man-made, is not limited to the immediate loss of life. The reverberations continue for a very long time besides inflicting emotional and monetary trauma on the victims of such disasters. The role of insurance companies becomes very important in such a situation in order to reduce the economic repercussions of such disasters. ICICI Lombard has time and again operated with the understanding of this huge responsibility.

For example, the train bombings in Mumbai on July 11, 2006 brought with it unprecedented loss of life and property. Apart from property-related claims, ICICI Lombard also received a substantial number of claims under the Personal Accident and Credit/Debit/ATM card policies. Majority of the claims were settled within 30 days from date of bomb blast. The average payout was Rs 4.5lakh per claim. While the company ensured prompt settlement of these claims, an earnest attempt was made to alleviate the suffering as the formalities were reduced to the minimum and requirement of documents were restricted to just mandatory ones. Similarly, in the wake of the terror attack on star hotels in Mumbai on 26 November 2008, the company made a payment of Rs1 crore within three days involving personal accident claims.

The above are among many such examples where the company has shown humane attitude in the settlement of the insurance claims whilst maintaining its efficient and professional stance and acting with utmost promptitude.

Bajaj Allianz : Quick settlement as their Work Culture

On 28 June 2007 REI Agro Ltd reported an inundation loss to their stock of paddy kept in the open covering 75 acres of land in Haryana with an estimate of Rs.74.75 crore. Bajaj Allianz immediately appointed the surveyors from Delhi. In order to monitor loss minimization and salvaging operations, Delhi claims department was advised to attend the site along with the surveyors. In consultation with surveyors and head office claims department, the insured deployed additional manpower for faster segregation of undamaged stock and started looking for a salvage buyer. The quantity being huge, it took almost 70 labourers working 24 hours for this activity. Finally the loss was quickly negotiated with the clients at Rs.3.5 crore which was about 5% of the estimate of loss. The survey report was received on 25 July 2007. Claim cheque of Rs 3.5crore was delivered on the 35th day of the loss.

A Bajaj Allianz official says that such speedy settlement is not an exception but a routine feature in the organization to ensure customer satisfaction and superior quality services in settlement of claims. Bajaj Allianz always strives for a win-win situation for both insured and insurer and thus demonstrates genuine interest by effective and speedy service to mitigate the loss suffered by the insured. The other interesting aspect was the deployment of additional manpower to ensure that the salvage segregation was fast so that the loss could be minimized to the maximum extent

IFFCO–Tokio:Concerned for the Customer

Sometimes in October 2004 a consignment of second hand machinery was travelling from UK to India belonging to Bharat Forge Limited, Pune valued at Rs 24.75 crore. BBC China, the ship carrying the consignment was caught up in rough weather and started sinking 1.5 nautical miles from South African Coast. The rescue team pumped out all the fuel through helicopters in order to avoid oil spill catastrophe but could not save the ship. The officials of IFFCO – Tokio monitored the event on day -to- day basis with great alertness, appointed an oversea surveyor for the lost consignment, rigorously followed up with the surveyor, got the report in a month's time and paid the entire amount of Rs 24.75 crore within 10 days from the date of receipt of the report, a kind of rare service every insured would crave for and no insured will ever forget. Not merely a positive mindset but the company officials should have that irresistible instinct for this kind of appropriate and quick settlement.

Unsung Heroism

Be it super cyclone in Orissa, be it earthquake in

Gujarat, be it Mumbai floods or be it the satellite not reaching its orbit, insurance companies have always risen to the occasion and have settled thousands of claims amounting to thousands of crore in record time and to the utmost satisfaction of the insured public, an act which though has not received due recognition from the society, is no less than any godly activity in terms of bliss. Agriculture Insurance Company of India alone pays claims to 6.3 million farmers annually- a feat that may appear incredible but verified as true. Perhaps the insurers believe that the only way to find your best self is to lose yourself in the service of others and in the process make your life a series of songs.

CHAPTER 2

Importance of Visiting the Site of Claim

"The journey of a thousand miles begins with a single step."
Lao Tzu

An accident to any insured property has the potentiality to generate an explosion of greed. It is but natural that uninsured and inflated portion of claims assessed and paid constitute a substantial part of our outgo. This is because we have assigned this central activity of business administration entirely to the outside agencies without our holistic supervision of the entire claim assessment process. It is mainly because of such insensitivity that at times other parties exploit the situation for their benefit. Instead of indulging ourselves in a variety of meaningless rituals we should focus ourselves more on our revenue- generating-and-loss-preventing tasks of claim management. Thus visiting immediately to the sight of claim is an opportunity we should grab with both the hands. It will not only activate our common sense but will open our eyes to the insight of knowing what is right and what is wrong. Thus visiting site should be our natural forte which will not allow any doubt nestling in the nether region of our mind during settlement. Here are some true tales that would appear stranger than fiction.

Ordinary visit: extraordinary Outcome

A huge fire was reported in a godown ,situated in Daman industrial area storing plastic moulded products like motor vehicle battery casings. The godown was insured for Rs 2 crore and the loss intimated by the insured was for Rs 1.85 crore. As usual the local office had appointed a local surveyor for preliminary survey. The cause of fire as reported by the preliminary surveyor was accidental drop of fire crackers on Diwali festival evening and three godowns of RCC constructions full of battery casings had been destroyed by this devastating fire and estimate of loss in his report was about Rs 1.85 crore.

Three days after the fire the claim management team visited the site and noticed to their utter disbelief that only one godown was of RCC and the rest two rather big ones were only temporary open sheds of wooden pillars with plastic tarpaulin as the roof. Falling of live fire crackers ignited the highly flammable plastic tarpaulin which ultimately dropped on the stock of plastic containers. Because of the highly inflammable nature of plastic containers, fire quickly spread and destroyed the materials in the RCC godown also.

Preliminary surveyor was advised to come and was asked to write the fact that only one godown was of RCC and the other two were of temporary sheds and only the RCC godown was insured under the policy. And he was kind enough to correct things without much resistance. The insured after arguments and counter arguments and with the intervention of the prudent final surveyor was finally convinced of accepting the compensation for the loss of materials inside the RCC godown only since the other two were the uninsured temporary sheds. The claim was finalized for Rs.41 lakh which, but for the visit by the underwriters, would have added the uninsured loss of Rs 1.44 crore of stock inside those two temporary sheds. This finding did not require special intelligence. By mere routine visit, one can save a lot by ascertaining what is insured and what is not.

Visit to nip it in the Bud

A printing press in Bhandup area was flooded due to collapse of a portion of boundary wall protecting the factory from the nearby drain consequent upon heavy rains. Loss intimated was Rs 1.25 crore for building machinery and stock. The insured had already taken one claim from the previous flood for Rs 79 lakh.

Preliminary surveyor had given a two page report stating that the factory premises was submerged under two and half feet of flood water. Machinery, stock and building had been severely damaged. Estimate of repair of machineries was awaited. Estimate of loss in his opinion too was Rs 1.25 crore.

Two days after the loss the claim management team visited the site and to their utter surprise there was no entry of flood water into the shop floor and all machineries were working to their full capacity without any trace of water mark thereon.

There was collapse of some portion of the boundary wall and some damage was done to the stock stored in the low-lying area of the factory premises. Some of the stocks stored inside temporary sheds were also damaged which the final surveyor did not take into assessment.

When contacted, the preliminary surveyor corrected himself saying that there were two and half feet of water in the factory compound and not in the factory premises, which was written through oversight. Factory premises and shop floor had been built on an elevated platform of a new building so designed from the experience of the previous flood which couldn't be affected even if the compound was flooded. The surveyor rectified his report with a big "apology" note. The claim, which was considered only for stock and the boundary wall, was assessed for Rs 25 lakh and was paid within a month's time much to the happiness of the Insured who got the right indemnity at the right time. All is well that ends well. But it does not always happen that way because of our not visiting the site of claim in time.

Unbelievable but True

Exactly nine months after the date of fire, the survey report was handed over to an assistant in the branch office by the loss assessors. The concerned assistant knew nothing of the claim, thus dumped it into oblivion. One month thereafter when the insured came and enquired about the claim, the report was ferreted out and was found with an assessment of Rs 1.15 crore, being the value of chemicals destroyed by fire.

On enquiry, it was found that since the claim intimation did not mention the estimate of loss, the divisional office presumed the loss to be around Rs 5 lakh and appointed the surveyor and forgot. The learned surveyors on their part neither bothered to give a preliminary report nor a rough estimate of loss for provisioning for reasons best known to themselves. After studying the photographs and counting the damaged 50 kg bags of dry chemicals therein the Claim Management Team (CMT) would know for sure that assessment was highly inflated. Even though it was very late, it was decided that claim management team should visit the site of claim alongwith BO/DO team, the insured's team, and the team of surveyors. It was noticed that damaged dry chemicals in 50 kg bags stocked in heaps in the affected godowns were burnt but the burnt stack had remained intact as per the photographs taken by the surveyors at the time of survey ten months back. The team along with the surveyors started physically counting the stock of burnt bags. The godowns were of the size of 16' x 46' although surveyors had measured them as 25'x 65' and such heaps were few and were countable.

The liquid chemicals in drums were also damaged and all the damaged drums (steel and plastic) were there as per the photographs and were compared. The type and number of chemicals in bags and drums were recorded and signed by all the concerned parties.

The loss assessors had calculated the loss of 6000 bags whereas in physical verification the Team found only 998 bags in all the stacks and neither there was any sign of nor space for the storing of such huge quantity of 6000 bags. When calculated as per the rates provided by the insured, the claim was reduced from Rs 1.15 crore to Rs 25 lakh.

A Stitch in Time

There are obscure places in suburbs of Mumbai where identification of godowns storing various merchandise is a perennial problem. Therefore, when the insurance office received intimation that a godown containing readymade textile goods worth Rs 40 lakh had been completely engulfed in fire, the claim management team swung into action and rushed to the site alongwith a policy copy which had covered the insured's godown no. 9.

On arrival the team found that insured and his team are talking in whispers. But immediately the cat came out of the bag and it was known to one and all that insured's godown no.6 had been damaged by fire. Although identification of 6 was not very clear but godowns no. 9 was verified to have been unaffected. And the insured was trying to manage police report and fire brigade reports in favour of godown no. 9 being damaged by the said fire.

Immediately, the team appointed an investigator over phone and instructed him to insure that he obtained fire brigade and police report in favour of godown no. 6 which had actually been damaged by fire. The office did not repudiate the claim but gave an option to the insured to withdraw the same. If he insisted for the claim, not only his claim would be repudiated but his policy would be cancelled just as well. The insured was convinced and withdrew the claim of uninsured losses with a note of sadness.

Differentiating Stacking from Dumping

The insured had three separate fire and allied peril policies: one for the flour mill, one for the rice mill and third one for the oil mill although these three mills were housed in the same premises. When cyclone hit his factory complex, the divisional manager thought there would be three separate claims; hence individually each one of them would come within his financial limit for settlement. Three months after, the technical department confirmed that these three would be treated as one claim since the occurrence was one, location was one, and the insured was one.

The claim management team visited the factory (which had started normal production by then) and found thousands of wheat bags of 50 kg each were arranged in stack and kept in open space. The situation provoked the CMT into thinking and when asked why he did not construct a solid roof and walls for storing this stock, the insured replied that feng sui did not favour the construction of a building over here.

It was symptomatic to refer to the claim file already submitted by the surveyor. The team found the photographs of similar stock of thousand bags in wet condition stacked in the same manner at the same place. When asked, the surveyor said that these bags of wheat were damaged by cyclonic rains while stored inside the factory premises and were taken out in damaged condition and dumped outside and the same had been included in the assessed amount of the loss. The argument of CMT was that once the bags were rain damaged, they would be twisted and could not be stacked in another place in a symmetrical manner as shown in the photograph. They could only be haphazardly dumped. The stacked bags in the photograph were covered with polythene sheets before and were torn by cyclone. Otherwise, why should the cyclone-damaged-dumped-bags need to be covered by large torn polythene sheets? It was proved beyond doubt that the huge stocks of wheat while in sound condition were stocked outside the factory premises before the cyclone which were clearly not covered under the policy. As confirmed during our visit, it was the practice of the insured to store wheat bags in the open during non-monsoon period and cyclone had hit in the last week of October. After a lot of arguments, the surveyor admitted the lapses and revised his report deleting thousands of bags from his assessment.

Common Sense and Lab Test

An explosion occurred in a godown on the ground floor in the industrial estate. The insured's manufacturing unit was situated on the 3rd floor. The impact of the explosion was so severe that it somehow affected the properties of the insured lying on the third floor. As a matter of loss control measure, the insured had shifted the damaged machinery and stocks to his own nearby factory premises and had claimed Rs 50 lakh towards the heat damage of the raw materials consisting of electronic components.

The claim management team visited the site and observed during inspection of the stock that the raw materials were well packed in polythene bags. The store manager of the insured confirmed that the stocks were lying in the same bags at the affected location during the occurrence of fire and explosion. The team further observed that these delicate polythene bags were absolutely intact and had not undergone any damage such as melting and crumpling as it should have been if these were subjected to even negligible heat. Hence there could not be any physical damage to the stocks. The insured therefore was informed to carry out testing of these items and submit the report. The insured tried to be evasive saying that the items were damaged because of being very delicate nature. After a series of arguments and counter arguments, he finally tested the sample components in his own laboratory and every thing was found to be intact. Hence in view of this, the insured withdrew the entire claim on raw materials of his own.

Finding Clue to the Truth

A huge fire was reported from the insured dealing with synthetic yarn and clothes with an estimated loss of Rs 2.38 crore. The Claim Management Team (CMT) rushed to the spot and smelt something fishy and recommended the appointment of a prudent surveyor. The surveyor after his visit signalled that the estimate had been highly exaggerated. Seven months passed in scrutinizing piles of documents by the surveyor. The insured mounted pressure on higher management through his consultants for quick settlement. Before the claim stumbled into controversies the CMT leader during a meeting with the insured took him into confidence and asked for the following information. A = stock as on 1 April 2006. B = stocks purchased from 1 April 2006 till 6 June 2006 that is date of fire. C = stocks sent out for dying during this period. D = stocks sold during this period.

He gave these details in four separate letterheads duly stamped and signed. When calculated the result was (A+B) – (C+D) = Rs 24 lakh of stock available at the time of fire as per insured's own statement. But the insured was not ready to accept despite the learned surveyor also arriving at the same amount. The CMT fished out series of photographs of the damaged stock showing that the stocks of synthetic goods were stored all over the hall in small pyramids. As in the photograph, how come only top portion of the pyramids could be damaged by fire as also was noticed by them during the visit? How was it possible for the accidental fire to burn only top portion of each pyramid? The insured sank inside himself in the face of truth and had no answer. Since the forensic report was favourable, it was difficult to reject the claim. Finally his bankers were convinced and the insured in turn was convinced by the bankers and accepted the amount of Rs 24 lakh towards full and final settlement.

Lessons from the Experience

Hard fraud refers to when someone invents a loss, say, by deliberately setting fire to his insured property. Such occurrences are few and far between. But claimant's exaggeration of otherwise genuine claims (which are known as soft frauds or opportunistic frauds) are no less frequent in the world of insurance. Again, the number of cases detected is much less than the number of cases committed. Today, when premium rates have bottomed out and high claim ratio is threatening industry's survival, we should abandon wasting time on trivial issues and participate actively in claims management. Visiting the claim site means: we came, we saw and we found the truth and prevented the bitter dispute that would have erupted between the surveyor and the insured. This is not for the benefit of the insurance company alone but for the insured community at large who otherwise have to bear the cost of such avoidably inflated claims in terms of higher premium payout.

A word about the Claim Management Team (CMT)

It is not that the mission of the CMT to be always fault finding. It aims at unearthing hidden gems of information to arrive at the right kind of indemnity and thereby eliminating unwanted beneficiaries. It has helped many an insured of genuine losses in getting their rightful claim in record time of three weeks. When the insured is so meticulous in inviting quotations, verifying rates and paying the premium which is so little, why can't we be equally meticulous in paying a claim which is quantum wise so huge. Therefore let us not hesitate to do quality control on our final product called claims. If the importance of instant visit to the site of claim by the insurance official is ignored as unimportant, it may grow into a Frankenstein monster. Scapegoating intermediaries will not be logical and company officials cannot be entirely blameless for such lapses. If nothing else, their visit will instil life to claims and give a quick start for settlement.

CHAPTER 3

"Reading, writing, studying art or paying attention to nature can all give your inner genius a bit of fuel to burn."

Impact of Bad Underwriting on Claims

It is famously said that Jesus Christ knew how to bring a dead man back to life.For example when Lazarus, a disciple of Jesus died, the sister of Lazarus kept his dead body in a cave. Jesus arrived three days after getting this sad news. Standing at the entrance of the cave Jesus said his prayers and called Lazarus to come out and a dead Lazarus came out alive. Two of his close disciples insisted that they be taught the secret.

Jesus said, "Once you are dead, you cannot apply it on yourselves" They pleaded that they wanted to apply it on others. Very reluctantly a pressurized Jesus gave them the secret.

Overwhelmed with joy they ran from village to village

in search of a dead body for application of the newly aquired secret. But they were disappointed because they got none. Finally, they found the mutilated parts of a skeleton at a village end and blinded by enthusiasm, they immediately applied the secret. Suddenly a furious lion got back to life and killed both of them instantly since it was the skeleton of a lion, which they could not visualize since they were in a great hurry. Similarly, the cost of paying claims is so much that the underwriters cannot accept proposals with wide-eyed blindness.

Court cases: Implicit admission of underwriting failure

Underwriting without complete understanding of the risk is equally hazardous. A slight mistake may land you in serious trouble and may cost your company a fortune. For example it was in March 1991 a reputed construction company approached a PSU underwriter for covering only "the staging and scaffolding" for a sum insured of Rs 24 lakh. For the reasons best known to the insured, the main civil work that was construction of Longai bridge in Assam was neither offered for insurance nor the underwriters of Guwahati office had asked for it. And a comprehensive cover was given under fire policy "building under construction" section. The underwriters exposed their underwriting shortcomings. Exactly forty-two days after the commencement of coverage a furious flood came and washed away the staging and scaffolding.

The surveyor assessed the loss for Rs 21 lakh but the underwriters started dragging their feet over the issue by neither paying nor denying the claim. First because how could they cover only scaffolding without covering the main project? Second because if the whole project cost was to be considered as value at risk, there was heavy underinsurance which surveyor had not taken into consideration. Third because definition of flood under fire policy is the presence of water at a place where it should not be. In this case the presence of flood water had been only in the river bed which was its natural presence Hence liability of the underwriters was debatable. Under a contractors all risk policy the story would have been different. The underwriters got trapped in the complicated relationship with the insured. Thus the stalemate continued and a sweeping melancholy followed. After waiting for three years, the insured in 1995 filed a complaint before National Consumer Dispute Redressal Forum. In 1997 the underwriters relented and offered Rs 21 lakh without interest towards settlement of the long pending controversial claim. The contractors rejected the offer outright. Finally in July 2003 the national commission pronounced the verdict that there had been inordinate delay in processing and finalising the claim which would mean the deficiency of service on the part of the underwriters. Hence the insureds were entitled for the claim amount plus interest at the rate of 18% per annum from the date of claim till the date of payment. The underwriters filed appeal in Supreme Court by spending further money on expensive lawyers and the case was finally dismissed in favour of the insureds. In May 2003 the underwriters paid Rs 34.72 lakh towards interest alone apart from paying the claim amount of Rs 21 lakh. On the surface it appears to be this much. But imagine the time wasted in fighting a legal battle for eight years. Imagine the fees paid to the advocates. Imagine the number of trips the officials might have taken to Delhi to attend court proceedings. A little care at the time of underwriting by saying a firm and polite no to cover scaffolding alone would have prevented this Himalayan blunder on the part of the insurance company. It is not merely loss of money and waste of time but the morbid feeling of being entangled in intricacies of the problem causes grievous injury to both the parties.

History repeats itself. But man does not learn from its repetition. The same contractors approached the same underwriters for insuring one pier of Passighat bridge under construction across the Brahmaputra river and the latter agreed and issued CAR policy and the said pier got tilted by the flood giving rise to insurance claim for Rs 18.35 lakh and the same problem cropped up and finally the insurance company had to pay Rs 18.35 lakh + interest @ 17.5% for Rs 37.75 lakh + cost of Rs. 10,000 as awarded by the supreme court. This was done with lots of discomfort. The moral of the story is that the whole project and not part of the project in isolation aught to have been insured.

Short Circuit and Fire Policy

Contribution of short circuit to the controversy of fire claims cannot be discounted. For example the divisional manager of an insurance company sold fire insurance covering smelter plant of Asia's biggest aluminum company and was happy to collect Rs 3 crore premium. He issued the fire policy and thought that the job was done.

Three months after, there was a fire in the plant damaging busbar system in all six legs of rectifier unit. The insured submitted an estimate of Rs 6 crore but the survey report indicated that the unit had been damaged due to heavy short circuiting and arcing. Since the total unit consisted of electrical items, the claim was outside the scope of fire policy. The same claim could have been paid under machinery breakdown insurance. The insured flared up into flames for not having been advised to cover the same under machinery insurance and declared with absolute finality not to renew the policy with the same company any further. The business and the customer relationship got lost forever.

The problem is once we get fire premium and issue a policy, we feel our underwriting job is over till the next renewal. But we should immediately write to the insured to cover his electrical equipments like circuit breaker, control panel and switch gear under machinery breakdown policy. This cover for all the machinery may be too expensive to afford but for selected coverage of electrical items which are more susceptible to short circuit should not be a problem. If the insured says no, it is a different story. But it is our duty to apprise him of the hazards involved in electrical equipment and how our fire policy does not cover that.

But for this, our relationship with the insured will be short circuited in case such situations arise which in fact do arise more often than not. As a Chinese proverb rightly says if you focus on results, you will never change, if you focus on change, you will get results.

The Insured as Underwriter

The greatest Chinese philosopher, Confucius had once said, "Disasters do not have instruction manuals. They can strike in a manner beyond all comprehensions and calculations of man." It is more applicable to insurance underwriting than anywhere else. Our proposal form duly filled in, pre-inspection conducted and reported by a qualified engineer, our quantification and assessment of burning cost leading to a recommended rate can be proved wrong by supernatural powers. War is too important to be left to the generals alone. Underwriting is too important to be left to the insured alone in taking decisions. If done so, it might have catastrophic consequences. For example, on 1 April 1989 the renewal of fire policy of a huge petrochemical industry was due. The sum insured was in thousands of crores and the premium was Rs 12 crore. Krishnan, the Director Finance of the company ,called Sengupta the divisional manager of the insurer and handed over a cheque of Rs 10.5 crore stating that they did not want flood, storm and tempest extension cover. Since there had not been any incidence of flood, storm and tempest for the past 15 years since the inception of the industry, there was no use paying Rs 1.5 crore towards covering such far-fetched perils. Sengupta, the pragmatic underwriter said, "Anything can happen anytime and it is not wise to take such a dangerous decision". Director Finance, a seasoned chartered accountant, wanted to save premium and impress his management on cost minimization, hence did stick to his point of view and all the persuasion and marketing skill of the divisional manager did have little effect. Finally, Sengupta said, "In that case, sir please give me in writing that you do not want flood, storm and tempest cover" and Director Finance obliged. Time passed and came the month of July bringing along a full- blown monsoon. The plant in question was situated on a valley mountain- ringed on three sides. During heavy rains the excess water used to flow out through the open side. But unknown to the director finance, the newly constructed Konkan railway line had blocked the passage of water through the open side. In July that year there was unprecedented rainfall, and small sluice gates underneath the railway line were not big enough to drain out the accumulation of rain water due to torrential rainfall. Thus, the entire factory got submerged under 10 feet of water causing an estimated loss of Rs 200 crore generating tremendous tension for both the parties. But the letter from the insured asking in writing to delete the flood, cyclone and tempest covers from the renewal absolved the underwriters from the liability of compensating the huge loss. Thus the knowledge of the risk manager should not be confined to the risk covered but should be extended over the geography of the area in which the risk is situated. The underwriters would have been happy to pay such catastrophic losses. But it was unfortunate that the risk could not be assessed in its proper perspective either by the insurer or by the insured. The clearly avoidable tragedy cost Krishnan his job, the Insured, their claim and the underwriters their long-standing business relationship.

Application of Intuition in Underwriting

A consignment of software was dispatched from Mumbai to Malaysia meant for core banking solutions of a major bank of that country and was declared for insurance for an agreed value of Rs 1 crore. It was dispatched by air. A fortnight after, National Insurance Company in Mumbai received an intimation of non-delivery claim of the entire consignment. The surveyor submitted the report for Rs 1 crore with relevant documents including the non-delivery certificate from the concerned airlines. Ganeshan, the chief manager-in-charge of claims while scrutinizing the claim file applied his intelligence. On enquiry, he could know that what had been dispatched as a consignment of software was nothing but a CD costing Rs 60 only, the back up of which was available in the form of another CD. After a long stretch of arguments and counter arguments the stormy claim was finally assessed for Rs 60. But a little more into details at the time of acceptance would have saved all the trouble. And had the intuitive chief manager like Ganeshan not been there, the claim might as well have got paid.

Let Overturning cover be Inbuilt

For the equipment like excavators, cranes and bulldozers operating on hilly areas or at uneven grounds, the major risk involved with such kind of vehicles is Overturning. Sometimes the insured intends to cover them under motor policy instead of usual comprehensive contractors plant and machinery policy. The insurance companies unfortunately use truck proposal forms to underwrite such specialized vehicles. The truck proposal does not ask the prospective insured whether he wants overturning cover or not. This overturning coverage is not inbuilt in the basic cover and hence has to be taken by paying an additional premium of 0.50%. But more often than not, the insured thinks that he has taken full coverage by paying 1.25% basic premium but in reality he has not been given the coverage that is very vital.

But the irony is that most of the accidents to such vehicles take place due to overturning considering the hazardous nature of work and more hazardous area of operation. Hence such claims run into troubled waters because the underwriters refuse to pay in the absence of add-on cover of overturning which is available only on payment of additional premium. Such problems have remained unsolved for decades. It is suggested that either a separate proposal form be devised to cover such vehicles with a specific column for overturning coverage or the overturning should be inbuilt in the basic cover in order to have peaceful settlements of claims because such proposals come very occasionally and it is not possible on the part of the agent or development officer all the time to remember to charge 0.50% and include overturning cover. It is therefore in the fitness of things that this be included in the basic cover by merging the overturning premium with the basic premium. This arrangement will bring immense grace to our customer relationship management.

Lessons for the Future

Looting through rioting by a mob after flood and cyclone is excluded under fire policy. It is not covered under our burglary and house breaking policy either. When such claims were rejected in Odisha and West Bengal, parties approached National Consumer Dispute Redressal Forum and got the redressal in their favour on the ground that they have taken both the policies and hence should not be deprived of their rightful claim. Now the point is why cannot the underwriters give an option to the insured to cover this under fire policy by charging additional premium when they are ultimately paying such claims. Let us not delay further in rising to the occasion.

Let us give it a Kick-start

We arrange conferences at hill stations on peripheral issues like accounts, audits, vigilance, official language implementation and target fixation in star hotels. But little do we care to have a conference on effective underwriting and judicious management of claims despite the fact that these two functions are central and vital to the very success of our business administration especially when most companies are operating with a combined ratio of more than 120 per cent. It is largely through such conferences that the causes of bad claims experiences can be identified, analysed, shared and then utilized as input - lessons for building a sound underwriting model for the   future.

It is wrong to think that insurance companies are rich, fat and would not miss a few hundred crores. The inside story is that most of the general insurance companies both public and private are incurring huge underwriting losses. Only time will tell how long they are going to survive eating out of their precious capitals and reserves. It is not a rude wake up call to insurance underwriters but a polite reminder to them to remain alert and awake because effective underwriting will be the best balm to heal the bleeding balance sheets. Moreover rejecting a wrong claim is something that does not always end peacefully.

CHAPTER 4

We need to surround ourselves with quality human beings that are intelligent and have a vision.

Preventing Leakages: Ways and Means

The underwriting losses have been jumping to unbelievable heights with every passing financial year. These chilling results paint worrisome pictures of what is wrong in the system and give a wake up call for the PSU general insurance companies to see the writing on the wall, think and find out solutions with absolute urgency. The speed and severity of the downturn took many people by surprise because it is the highest loss recorded ever. The cat is already out of the bag and the truth is that some of the PSU companies are conducting business with 132% combined ratio, which in common man's language means while income is Rs 100, the outgo is Rs 132. Such results make a very disturbing reading indeed. If we keep losing Rs 4,600 crore a year, time will not be far off when we will have nothing left to lose any more.

Therefore, our objective should be keen and focused in matters of reducing combined ratio to an acceptable limit. The prime method to achieve this objective is to feel concerned. Only when we are concerned, we can visualise solution. Much may not be done in reducing management expenses but more can be done in controlling claim costs which generously contribute to underwriting losses and can bankrupt insurance companies.

Visiting claim sites : Great leap forward

Claims are the final products of the insurance company. Any company's financial health and reputation in the market depend on efficient and judicious settlement of claims. Such a vital activity should not be left entirely to the outsourced agency. Our property claims are managed by surveyors, liability claims by lawyers and health claims by TPAs who are not as accountable for their errors of omissions and commissions as our employees.

In a study conducted among the hundred of participants from four PSU companies, it was revealed that leakages in claims are to the tune of 20% by a conservative estimate which means thousands of crores go down the drain every year. To tackle this, companies can form the Claims Management Team (CMT) choosing **intelligent, dedicated, honest and enthusiastic** people to do this most important job. They should along with the department officials visit the site of claim, make a conscious effort to take inventory of the loss, follow up for documents and discuss with both the surveyor and insured to arrive at the assessment of loss and stay engaged till the claim is settled. This has been tested and experimented resulting in an automatic reduction of claim cost by as much as 30%. And this is by mere visit. More can be achieved by putting in intelligent and sincere application with a view to reducing delay and arriving at right amount of assessment.

Take for example - A consignment of medicine was despatched from Mumbai to Goa by a truck and was insured with Tata AIG valued at Rs 50 lakh. It collided with another truck in Goa and the consignment got damaged. It was the monsoon month of July and thus the insured panicked and intimated to the underwriters in Mumbai. Immediately two officials of Tata AIG along with the surveyor took the earliest flight to Goa, hired a godown, segregated the undamaged from the damaged truck in the presence of a drug inspector and the loss was assessed on physical verification then and there for Rs 35,000 only. The insured accepted the assessment and got most of his consignment saved . This is one of the many examples as to how claims are handled in private sector. Why can't we be more like them to manage claims and ensure underwriting profit?

Thus regional heads may be given the primary task of minimising losses and generating profit. With tariff disappearing and market slowly becoming broker driven, they have all the time in the world to visit the site of high value claims to have a look at the extent of damage in its original form rather than depending on the second hand and interpreted version of the surveyors. In short, assessment of loss is a vital financial activity and therefore to leave it to outsource agency alone would amount to an explosion of irresponsibility.

Diverting part of audit team to Claims Management Team.

Audit team is synonymous with a group of extraordinarily talented people. But the kind of efforts they are putting in checking volumes of documents and hundreds of activities are hard labour lost without producing desired results.

Therefore part of manpower of audit may be utilized for claim management. With the tariff regime gone, underwriting has become liberal. If 60% of manpower in present system of audit doing the dull and routine check up is diverted to form claim management team, say, two persons in each regional office, there certainly will be a turnaround in company's profit and loss account which at the moment is in the red. If they visit the site of claim, apply their basic intelligence, utilize their experience and participate actively in claims assessment, companies will most certainly regain their lost financial health. These esoteric few thus selected can do wonders if they have the capacity to generate interest, the willingness to know and the necessary conviction for execution of one of the most assured objectives of management – increasing shareholders' value through cutting claims costs.

Instead of chasing the recovery of smaller amounts of money as they are doing at present, this way they can erase the impression that the assessment of claims are usually inflated. They too can prevent people taking collateral benefits from such claims.Like the proverbial alchemist's stone, this arrangement will turn baser metals into gold and stave off claim worries of the company. The instinct for improvisation is inside everyone of us. We have only to stimulate it.

Auto tie-up: Let them not take us for a Ride

This is another area where companies are bleeding profusely. We release payouts to the dealers to the tune of 40% on premium received and pay claims inflated to the tune of 40% as compared to repair expenses in outside garages. What benefits do the insurance companies get out of it is a million dollar question. If a company receives a premium of Rs 900 crore and pay claims amounting to Rs 1,300 crore, it is most unbusiness like. It is believed that auto-dealers make more money from insurance than from their own business of selling motor vehicles.

We should sign agreement dealer-wise on profit sharing basis keeping management expenses at the back of our mind. Surveyor should be appointed by the insurance officials on case-to-case basis and must not be picked up by the dealer from the panel. Reviewing the performance of surveyors constantly is necessary to less utilize the more expensive ones. With so much of loss ratio the insurance company is at a better bargaining position to pull out of the tie-up when it feels suffocating. This is the 21st century and business is done with profit and not with charity. The reason, the existence for any modern business organization, is primarily reasonable operating surplus. And it is high time that we realised this fundamental economic principle.

Third Party Administrator

With their very existence claims are inflated by the hospitals. It is because of TPA's involvement and cashless settlement, hospitals come to know about the patient's Insurance Cover and inflate the bill even to the tune of 100% at times. There should be provision that if the Insured is willing for reimbursement mode settlement, he should be given 25% to 30% discount in premium with an advice not to disclose to the hospital that he is insured. The leakge ratio will considerably come down.

Implementation of the very TPA system contributes huge share of loss to insurance companies. Insurance companies have money and men enough to run their in-house TPAs which will bring down the claim ratio drastically. At least the company will not have to pay TPA fees which are in crores in addition to huge load of claims, agent's commissions and brokers' fees.

Act to replace MACT: a much-needed amendment

Jeremy Bentham, who was the proponent of utilitarianism, once said, law of the land should be made for doing the greatest good for the greatest number of people. If this is true, the concept of MACT is untrue and not beneficiary friendly. The settlement ratio of TP claims is much less compared to claim pending and claims filed. There are 12 lakh cases pending pertaining to PSU companies alone amounting to Rs 16,000 crore of public money waiting for decades to be paid to the beneficiaries out of which, more than 99 percent are related to the poor, destitute and helpless.

The claim ratio in TP is far beyond hundred percent which is a major contributing factor for underwriting losses. In a recent road accident in Goa 15 NRIs have died and each one of them has claimed Rs.10 crore towards compensation in MACT, Surat. For a premium of Rs 4,000/- which the concerned vehicle owner had paid, no insurance company will survive if such huge liability of Rs 150 crore arises in a single accident. The only way to bring a solution to this huge problem is to make the compensation structured irrespective of person's earning capacity say Rs. 10 lakh for death of an adult and Rs 5 lakh for a child below 18 years of age. Insurance companies may be empowered to settle such claims directly after getting legal heir certificates and without complicated procedure of going through the court. The rich, which constitute much less than one percent of MACT claims, have enough money for their future and do not have to entirely depend on third party compensation. The poor in turn will get hassle free benefit without paying fat fees to intermediaries like lawyers. Injury cases can be calculated as per Workmen's Compensation Act. This will relieve the insurance company of a back-breaking load of TP claims and will also benefit millions of families with compensation money at a time when they need it most. Under the suggested system, there would be less of manipulation and no filing of bogus claims. It is a sincere appeal to our lawmakers to take notice of this precarious situation and bring about a bill in the parliament authorising insurance companies to pay this simple and rightful compensation directly thereby doing good to the maximum number of countrymen. This will in turn save the lawyers fees on either side because services of learned advocates are not required for such simple matter of claiming and receiving rightful payments. If this is not done, the problem will remain unsolved for next the hundreds of years.

Orphan claims: search for the real parents

The matter is very simple and the solution simpler. When the identities of the insured and the vehicle in the accident are known, only the insured may be directed to produce the policy copy or else pay the compensation. But the matter gets complicated by asking a particular insurance company to prove that they have not issued any such policy covering the vehicle in question only because the said company's name is mentioned in police documents as the insurer. Under such circumstance we should conduct investigation on the insured and move an application in Tribunal to get the policy particulars from the insured, failing which company's name may be appealed for deletion from the list of defendants. But in reality we remain indifferent for years and suddenly one day judgment copy arrives directing us to pay such claims.

Then it hits us like a war missile during peacetime and we are not able to do anything despite knowing that the policy is not ours.

Eternal vigilance is the price of liberty. It is also the price of being both efficient and effective. Our advocate should be vigilant and we should be more vigilant. We should have a special cell defusing such claims before they reach flash points.

More often than not, we land up paying such claims that should have been paid by the vehicle owner for not taking an insurance policy. And unfortunately such claims are many and make a big dent in our balance sheet and all such uninsured people go scot-free transferring their liability to us. Let us put in ten times more effort not to allow this to happen any more and it should be done with a missionary zeal.

Vigilance process: a cure that aggravates illness

It is true both for the company and for the employee. There are more than 700 cases pending in each company for several years, which means these seven hundred odd people have been debarred from holding responsible assignments but entitled to take their full salary for years. A case of fraud in insurance company is simple one and can be inquired into within three sittings, a short but comprehensive report can be prepared during this period and thereafter the competent authority can pronounce judgment. But usually, it takes years and company loses not only in terms of wasted man-hours and money but also in terms of the revenue and value that could have been generated from the delinquent employees.

Once a case is registered, the management stops giving important work and employee almost stops working whatever is assigned to him. Further wastage of man-hours was in the formalities of appointing Enquiry officer and Presenting officer and the former takes years in examining witnesses and giving a huge report on simple lapses. The system in a way adopts a complicated way of solving simple problems. Proof lies in the fact that large number of cases are pending for a number of years and the number keeps increasing every year. Employee loses but company loses more in the process. Vigilance can play a more meaningful role in company affairs by simplifying the process of enquiry and quickening the process of delivering judgment. The department can observe vigilance clearance month during which most of the cases can be cleared.

Once vigilance cases are cleared, this huge manpower will be available and be utilised for company's mainstream of activity thereby increasing productivity.

Official language: a project that needs direction

We have been implementing Hindi as official language

for the last three decades. Officers who were recruited as Hindi officers have been promoted as DMs / Sr DMs. Hindi has moved into the heart of non-Hindi speaking people more through TV and Movie than otherwise. It should not take so many years to teach Hindi to existing employees.

Language does not get transmitted through compulsion but by creating a willing group of receptive people. To make language travel to an alien land, its literature, poetry and song should travel first. However much we may try, Hindi may not successfully get taught through this method because it is aggressive and not receptive. The more effective method would be to translate classics of regional languages to Hindi and translate works like Kabir's poetry and novels of Premchand into regional languages so that Hindi can travel to the heart of non-Hindi speaking people like a fountain travelling through rocky roads.

Again posting Hindi officers in Hindi speaking areas like Delhi, Lucknow, Kanpur, Bhopal, Jaipur and Patna is like carrying coal to New Castle. It is a colossal waste of manpower and money. When we are making so much of underwriting losses, we can assign official language implementation job in these regions as an additional portfolio to any of existing employees without incurring additional expenditure of recruiting separate Hindi Officers.

Frequent transfers: a dent in the human capital

Transfers cost money to the company. Transfer for the sake of transfer costs more money. Employees benefit by way of getting transfer grant twice (going to a new place and coming back after completing a few years during which he exhausts all the leave at his disposal). Companies gain nothing but only get the satisfaction of following rules and regulations. But at what cost? Man is a strange machine. He works effectively only when he is happy. Let us realise this and take the advantage of this universally accepted principle. Instead of transferring them en masse, let us take into account both the requirement of the company and willingness of the persons so that right man is posted at the right place for greater interest of the employee and the employer. If we take care of the balance sheet of human capital, the financial balance sheet will take care of itself.

Narayana Murthy has rightly said, "Everyday in the evening when my core corporate assets leave the office, me and my management team lose our sleep on how to get them back to the office next morning." Let the thoughts of this great man be a source of inspiration for our HR management because our people are our greatest assets.

Curbing of expenses to reduce combined ratio

Authorities may re-visit the decision on commission structure. Business like mediclaim which is generating huge load of losses should be dis- incentivised by way of no commission. Nobody in the world with little business sense will allow this in his business be it personal or corporate. And why should the insurance companies pay brokerage when underwriting losses of such portfolio are eating into their reserves accumulated painstakingly by their forefathers by sheer dint of their insight and hard labour?

Survey fees especially for fire claims should be rationalised. The principle of more assessment more fees should be replaced by a more scientific scale of pay especially when fire premium has been revised downwards

many times over since July 1987 and has hit the rock bottom at present. Sur veyors are partners in this business. They should not mind this downward revision for the sake of survival of the industry.

Of all the tours and travels undertaken, less than one percent pertains to visiting site of claims. With advanced communication facilities in place many of the things can be done without undertaking tours except risk inspection and claim management, which are our main business activity and where our presence is essentially necessary to see and to believe. Why do not we give it a kick-start right now and overcome from this grave crisis of underwriting losses.

Cutting down layers to reduce delay

Delay is the greatest epidemic that the companies are plagued with. Reputation of the companies is tarnished despite their paying the rightful compensation because they delay it beyond tolerance limit. For a claim of Rs 5 crore, 15 signatories are required from branch, division, region and head office. Nobody knows what is inside the file except the insured and the surveyor because those who put their autographs never visit the site of claim to see the original damaged insured property. They rely on assessment of the surveyor which is only an individual's point of view which may sometimes be outright wrong and sometimes not right enough. If we pay quickly, the mind of the insured will not be corrupted to take advantage of the mishap and inflate his claim. To overcome the layer problem, large claims should be assigned to a special group of dedicated people to complete the formalities and ensure fast-track settlement.

Training: making it more down to earth

Tata AIG recruits graduates and sends them to Tata Motors, Pimpri. Each candidate is given a Tata Indica car and a tool-box. He has to dismantle and reassemble the whole car in three months time and then only his training gets over. After that a man becomes a complete man so far automobile survey is concerned. What is needed is more and more practical training through visits to the claim site. No teacher is greater than practical experience. No knowledge can be compared to practical knowledge which our industry people have very little scope to acquire. The only people who get the benefit of training in the process are the surveyors because they anatomize hundreds of risks by hands-on experience, reading and re-reading the policy condition each time they are allotted survey job. All other trainings are horizontal but practical training is vertical and utilitarian. More focus should be given on such visits to sites of claims to enble the employees participate in the process of claim assessment in detail than making them read reports and sign claim notes.

Drivers' legal liability policy

In any road accident the driver is mostly to blame. Then why should the owner pay the compensation from his motor policy. Like any professional indemnity policy, the driver being a professional, he is also entitled to such a policy. It is high time that M. V. Act is suitably amended to make driver's legal liability policy compulsory. To begin with the driver should pay

Rs. 500 as premium to buy this policy and his policy should share 20% of the amount awarded against motor owner's policy for third party claims. His premium during renewal should go up by 20% with every accident caused by him and after three accidents his license should be suspended for six months. This arrangement will make the driver cautious and careful in future. Thus it will reduce accidents on the road. Since every driver will compulsorily be having this policy, the underwriters will get additional premium income to bring down the present alarming loss ratio and the vehicle owners will be able to verify the past records of the driver (since his license will be endorsed with each accident) before assigning him the job.

Mission possible

If Bajaj Allianz can settle a project claim in Dubai in thirty days why can't the public sector companies ? If Tata AIG can do claim minimisation why can't the PSUs? If Star Health can make profit in mediclaim why can't the PSUs? People who are working in those organisations are the people who were working with the PSUs. If they can generate sizeable underwriting profit why can't the PSUs? Before this problem snowballs into a crisis, let PSUs become pro-active and adopt some of the principles the private operators are implementing for better results. The PSUs have the potentiality, they have the time and yes, they can do it. Well, it is time to jolt this drowsing system to awake.

It is all in our hands

Long long ago there was an enlightened saint. A disciple came to him to imbibe the art of meditation and spiritual way of life. After three years of devotion, the disciple was put to test and came out successful in flying colours. The saint was very happy. While taking leave, the disciple requested to test the divine knowledge of his Guru. The Guru agreed. Hiding something in his hand the disciple asked 'Sir tell me, what is in my hand?'. The saint closed his eyes, went into meditation for a while and said, 'It is a butterfly.' The disciple was surprised with the right answer but was in no mood to give up easily. Then holding the butterfly inside his fist he asked, 'Sir now tell me, if it is alive or dead?' He thought, 'If the Guru says it is alive, he will immediately press it dead. If he says it is dead, he will let it fly to prove the Guru wrong.' The saint again meditated for a while and said with a supreme smile, ' My dear child, alive or dead it is all in your hands.'

The profit and loss of the Company is all in your hands–you the insurance officials.

CHAPTER 5

Talent hits a target, no one else can hit.
Genius hits a target no one else can see.

Motor Theft Claims and Application of Intelligence

Down the ages the claim intimation letter has been an insignificant document in the world of claim management. People who still think so need a reality check. Take for instance in motor theft claim it is vital and more so, when it is a case of close proximity. It is because various information in the intimation letter are insured's own and are given by the insured himself. More often than not, they are written in his own handwriting and he cannot go back denying the same. But unfortunately intimation letter as a document does not fire up any focused interest among claim officials despite the fact that this can provide proof enough to reject a bogus claim.

Invariably the claim manager attaches the least importance to this document and goes on investigating in every conceivable direction. Result: they land up with the often-repeated cliché that case is true but no clue which fits into the bill of settling a claim.

In some offices we have a printed format that the insured fills in for claim intimation, giving only impassioned information, which allows the mala fide claimant to reveal the superfluous and conceal the vital. Mostly, in a bogus claim intimation, the language would be evasive, the tone faltering, narration of the event haphazard and the time between the occurrence of theft and lodging of FIR too short to make it possible. The intimation in some cases, though is written by the insured himself, the FIR is written by someone else just to safely keep himself away from the police. In fabricated cases the statement of facts provided in intimation, FIR and claim form would substantially differ if read between the lines, which are never read meticulously. Way back in 1988, AGM Delhi RO telephones to divisional manager, Bhubaneshwar to quickly settle a car theft claim. The latter was totally unaware of the case and assured the AGM to look into the matter on priority basis. In the meantime, as a matter of coincidence, the DM was introduced to the concerned insured at common client's office which the insured was auditing as a CA. After the brief introduction the DM looked straight into his eyes and asked how could he know AGM, Delhi RO? The insured avoided eye contact and started sinking into the guilt corner of his mind and was instantly caught in the web of prima facie suspicion.

Time as the Deciding Factor

This incident led to the study of the intimation between the lines which read as follows: "I went to see off my wife in Konark Express. I had parked my car outside the railway station at 6.00 pm and after seeing off my wife when I returned at 6.10 pm, I found my car missing". FIR was scrutinized and it was found that GRP had acknowledged receipt of FIR at 6.30 pm. The train timing was 5.55 pm and since Bhubaneshwar was the starting point of the train, it always used to leave right in time. Railway authorities in writing confirmed that the last boggy on that particular day left the station at 5.59 pm. Hence it was impossible for his wife to have boarded the train later than that. And in a matter of few minutes it was impossible for someone to steal the car because 38 years back Bhubaneshwar was a country hick and perhaps it had never experienced a car theft ever before. Moreover he noticed his car missing at 6.10 pm and lodged FIR at 6.30 pm. In the duration of mere twenty minutes, it was impossible for the insured to look for the car, to reassemble his psyche which must have been shattered due to mishap-induced trauma, to walk to the police station, to narrate the incident, ask for the paper, write down the incident and get it acknowledged. It was possible only if FIR had been fabricated earlier at home.

Since the intimation and FIR were his very own documents, circumstantial evidences were strong enough to repudiate the claim.

A week later, a friend of the insured narrated his adventure, which breathed a fresh lease of life to the whole episode. The fact was that he had purchased his car from Goa by paying less octroi and had forgotten to insure the same out of the sheer excitement of possessing a new car. Two months after the purchase, the car got stolen from Berhampur, then he came to Bhubaneshwar and through a reputed dealer of Premier Padmini managed a fresh cover note for insurance giving the impression to the concerned development officer that he was taking the car from the same dealer. Ten days thereafter staged a drama that his car got stolen from Bhubaneshwar railway station.

Field force in PSU Insurannce Companies are too busy to physically verify the vehicle, more so when it happens to be a new one. The proposal forms are too obsolete to ask the date of purchase and compare it with date of insurance. Hence they sometimes land up in giving coverage to something they know nothing about and compensate a full amount when no loss having taken place during policy period.

Unlocking the Truth with the Second Key

Another such case happened on the seashore of Puri 30 years back. It was theft of a Maruti Zen. Within twenty minutes the car had disappeared and within next twenty minutes the FIR was lodged. In a small town like Puri stealing a bike would be difficult, let alone a car. This car was under hire purchase agreement. The financiers who were giving a crore of rupees premium were neither ready to buy our story of repudiation nor ready to accept that although the car pertained to another city and it did not have the evidence that it had gone through a toll gate, it was supposed to have passed through to come to the site of theft. And the office had the evidence that it had not passed at all. The financiers gave an ultimatum of sorts, 'Settle or produce concrete evidence or else the whole business would be shifted'. The office went into thinking ways and means to find a solution and on scrutiny it was found that the insured had surrendered one key only and the other one was with the financier. The second original key from the financiers was called for. And to our shock and surprise it was totally differ ent! Ultimately the financiers came round to our point of view. After a week an anonymous letter arrived from a well-wisher of the insured that the former had sold his car in Andhra Pradesh and was planning to take the insurance company for a ride.

The Grammar as a Clue

Usually bogus intimation letter contains a lot of loopholes that can be detected if read intelligently. But for some inexplicable reasons we simply hand over the case to the investigator and forget. And he does precious little because no brief and frame of reference is given to him. Here is one example how a bogus claim was detected early. The insured had parked his car at the city market and went to buy vegetables at 7:30 pm. At 8:00 pm he came back to find his car missing. Since the police station was just inside the market complex, the FIR was received by the police at 8:20 pm. The FIR read 'I went to the city market to buy vegetables. I had parked my vehicle outside the market at 7.30 pm. On returning at 8pm I saw it missing.' It was a break- in -insurance case. The insured had taken insurance three months after the expiry of the previous insurance. And seven days after the new insurance the theft was intimated. His residence was eight km away from the market. From the intimation it could be concluded that FIR was written at home. Had he written FIR at the place of incidence it would have been "I came to the market not I went to the market." The claim was repudiated.

What to Investigate

It happened in Kalina office of United India Insurance Company in Mumbai. Three strong men entered the Divisional Office of the insurance company and fished out three guns of different make and rested them on the DM's table asking for the immediate settlement of Maruti Zen theft claim pending for the last six months. The divisional manager started shivering in his shoes and said it had been sent to the regional office at Churchgate for sanction. On the visitors' pressure the DM telephoned to the regional manager and explained him the situation and got the reply that to-morrow by lunch time the claim would be settled. The leader of the visiting team snatched the receiver and shouted if by tomorrow it is not settled before lunch time we shall come to you with guns.

Next day at RO the file was scrutinized by the administrative officer who had joined his duty on that day after a long vacation. He noticed that a letter of no objection from Andheri Branch of the CS bank stating that although they were the financiers, 'they have no objection if the claim amount is paid to the owner of the vehicle.' The concerned officer was taken aback because his brother incidentally was working in that branch of the bank and that had been closed two years hence and had been shifted to Bandra. How can the insured produce a letter with Andheri address? The RM and his team of officials rushed to the bank and to their utter surprise learnt that the car has been confiscated by them due to non- payment of instalments. At lunch time the gun possessing insured phoned to the regional office for the claim and the reply given was that the RM and his team had gone to the CS bank for verification. Thereafter the phone from the gun-wielding insured never came. Now the question is what was the investigator doing. What did his eight page report contain?

More often than not, people do not apply their intelligence. They want documents like intimation letters and investigation reports just because they are necessary to avoid audit objection. They do not tell the investigator what aspects of the case he should investigate. When most of the general insurance companies are making huge underwriting losses and when premium rates have come down to all time low due to stiff competition, it is about time that they pulled up their socks and rise to the occasion. Money saved is money earned; now such claim repudiated is profit earned.

CHAPTER 6

Profiting from Losses

While I was having breakfast in a star hotel, the bearer carrying some empty plates mistimed his step and fell down. The breaking sound of falling plates sirened the entire restaurant staff to come running to the spot to enquire as to what happened. This small incident revealed that all of them were sincerely concerned about the loss of the employer even though monetarily it was a small loss. Contrary to this, when a huge loss occurs arising either out of a devastating fire in the factory premises or resulting from a flooded godown or in consequence of breakdown of the machineries, the underwriters show cold indifference to the insured's panicky call and consider that their duty is done and responsibility is over once they depute a surveyor who in turn neither has the accountability nor is concerned with the loss minimisation programme of the insurance industry.

Be the first to know

More often than not when left entirely to the surveyors, many things may happen which cannot be discussed in print but finally the claim runs into trouble waters. What the insurance company sometimes receives in the end is not usually the fact in original but an interpreted version in which the accuracy in assessment of loss succumb to many fallacies, either through human errors or through temptations to which man has a very poor resistance. Thus, the visit of insurance officials immediately to the site of loss should be the focused approach of underwriters who should ceaselessly monitor the survey and ensure that inventory is taken, relevant papers are obtained, the extent of damage is measured, valuation is done, depreciation and salvage are taken into account and the final amount is arrived at in one go and judicious conclusion is drawn which may include the client's consent.

With this kind of zero response time, the insurance companies will prevent fabrication of claims related to documentation and escalation of the amount of loss. It is said that a stitch in time saves nine. It is because insurance officials are indifferent in the beginning and do not associate themselves from the start of loss, they invariably draw foggy conclusions when the report is submitted along with the documents after a huge gap of time.

If they are sensitised to take interest by visiting the site of loss, it will not only reduce delay (to which the insured reacts with concentrated bitterness), but it will enhance customers' satisfaction thereby creating healthy atmosphere for insurance business transaction and will bring back the lost glory of insurance companies.

Wrong diagnosis: catch if you can

Way back in 1997, a consignment was dispatched from Russia via Delhi to an interior destination in Bihar pertaining to a public sector thermal power plant. It was insured overseas upto New Delhi. Overwhelmed by the intimate business relationship with the clients, the underwriters covered it under their declaration policy from New Delhi to clients' plant premises in Bihar without pre-dispatch inspection.

When the damage was reported at the destination, a junior surveyor was assigned the job, who reported that the loss would be huge. Hence, a senior surveyor was rushed to the spot, who assessed the loss for Rs 15 lakh, which the insured declined to accept and demanded total loss of the entire consignment of machineries, which was insured at an agreed value of Rs 35 lakh. Thus, a third surveyor was deputed and he increased the assessment by another Rs 10 lakh. Despite this enhancement, insured's finance department did not agree to the assessment.

In the meantime, it came to light that the consignment was lying for eight months at New Delhi airport before the tail -end- transit. Hence, the date and place of loss could not be ascertained. Since it was not pre-inspected before the acceptance, utter confusion and uncertainty followed. After the lapse of two years, there was pressure from top management of the insured on the top management of underwriters, hence the concerned senior regional manager from Patna visited the general stores of the clients and their general manager (materials) confirmed that the machineries could not be used only because the carbon brush was damaged, the cost of which was only Rs 1,500. The regional manager settled the claim on the spot and a cheque was handed over. From this real life incident, it can be concluded that left to the surveyors alone, assessment may not sometimes be authentic. This is not an isolated example. Many such instances go unnoticed through which huge amount of money evaporates thereby enhancing the emptiness of the insurance coffers.

RCC construction and misconception

Apart from wrong diagnosis of loss, another way by which leakages take place is the inflated assessment. Its disguising look is more hazardous than first perils. This can be prevented if insurance officials are alert and can study the assessment with intuition. One such inflated loss assessment and its dissection is discussed below.

The regional office deputed its officials to the site of a poultry firm which had collapsed due to a cyclone, received the report from renowned surveyors along with the assessment of Rs 26 lakh concerning civil works that constituted columns and beams which was calculated @ Rs 7,500 per cubic metre. On verification from the state public works department and local chartered civil engineers, it was ascertained that the market rate for each cubic metre of RCC was just Rs 3,500. Startled by the shocking anomalies the prudent claim officials wrote to the surveyors to give the specification of the quantity of materials required for every cubic metre of RCC. The reply received was 12 bags of cement, 24 bags of stone chips, 48 bags of sand, 100 kg of steel which was rationally unconvincing.

The matter was referred to various chartered civil engineers and state public works department who were unanimous in their opinion to say that it required 6 bags of cement , 12 bags of chips, 24 bags of sand

and 80 kg of steel. Since the surveyors had taken into account double the quantity of material barring the steel of course, the rate naturally was calculated almost twice that of the market rate. The matter was explained to the insured and he was nice enough to accept the fact. This might have been an error of judgment. But it is not always so. In fact, such assessments are never questioned. It is certainly a stupendous task. But you do not have to be a civil engineer to point out such tragedy of errors. Only if you love to take deep interest in analysing high value items intelligently, it may often be Eureka for your industry. The sad reality is that nobody ever bothers about the assessment. But how long can we afford to overlook this aspect when insurance companies are making losses with unerring regularity.

Common sense: how Uncommon

It is sometimes seen that even highly qualified surveyors arrive at assessment by using an accounting system which breaks all the boundaries of common sense. For example, an assessment by a chartered accountant surveyor received in respect of stolen sarees from a cooperative society for an amount of Rs 3,65,000 supported by impeccable study and analysis of insureds' books of accounts but when watchman's report was examined, it was found that only one trunkful of sarees were stolen. The concerned regional office sent an officer along with the surveyor to the site of loss and physically filled the trunk with the type of sarees alleged to have been stolen. When calculated, the cost of trunkful of sarees turned out to be just Rs 85,000.

There cannot be two opinions about the fact that knowledge is sometimes misused. Hence, one requires intuition to bring to light the cunningness of knowledge used for inflated assessment.

Attempting the impossible: Usually goes unnoticed

In 1998, a fire claim on generator transformer was put up for sanction with damaged interior parts replaced. A picture represents truth. Thus, a deep look at the photographs showed that even the exterior insulation claddings made mainly of cotton pads had hardly been damaged by fire. With this finding, the situation took a disturbing turn that led the underwriters to verify the invoice. Thus the claims department was clued into finding that the alleged spare parts costing Rs 12 lakh had been purchased in 1984 that was 14 years before the date of accident. Such costly spare part could certainly not wait for so long to be used. Thus, it was concluded without doubt that the parts had neither been damaged nor been replaced and more surprisingly, the surveyors finally consented to this logic and got the amount reduced in their report. The claims department understood the enormity of their achievement when the insured silently accepted the claim amount without protest. Such misleading situation would certainly not arise if trained claim minimization personnel of the company visit the site immediately after loss.

Insured's own statement: a clue often overlooked

A godown of wheat was looted after the cyclone. An FIR was lodged and intimation was given stating that hundreds of rioters looted the godown between 11am to 2 pm and took away the whole stock of Rs 50 lakh using bicycles and scooters.

The company officials made a visit next day and found the godown empty. The eminent surveyors made an assessment of Rs 35 lakh after verifying relevant books of accounts.

On scrutiny of the file, when the stock of Rs 50 lakh was calculated back to quantity of stock, it turned out to be total cost of 7,000 bags of 100 kg each, which was again equivalent to 70 truckloads.

The godown had one shutter and a subway and was situated downside of a highway 3 km away from the villages and thus it was impossible to loot 70-truck load in three hours duration and especially when the stock had been stacked up to 20-feet in height. This led to the verification of the alleged purchase of 5,000 bags immediately before the loss from FCI, which turned out to be false and therefore, it was confirmed that not more than 1,000 bags could be physically looted during three hours time, which was much less than what was claimed.

Therefore, it was convincingly proved that insured's intimation was immediate reaction to the situation, while the claim bill and documentation were his afterthought. Careful and intelligent study of claim intimation wordings is so very vital, but it is treated casually by the PSU companies, which ultimately aggravates the company's sorry state of financial condition.

In a very conservative estimate, small leakages in drops of 15 per cent on an average per claim make an ocean of Rs 3,000 crore going down the drain. It is the urgent need of present times that management of PSUs are required to revisit their decision on claim management plans and focus on minimization strategies.

Scope and exclusion: head-on collusion

The language in policy contracts are legalistic and the exclusions are by far too many, but the surveyors put their constant inattention to these and divert their entire attention to assessment only and do not point out whether a loss falls outside the policy, thereby voting in favour of the customer. For example, two trucks had head-on collusion at each other's drivers' seat killing driver of one tr uck and helper of the other. Circumstantial evidence proved beyond doubt that helper was driving one of the trucks whose driver had escaped unhurt since he was dosing off at helpers seat where the impact of the accident was the least.

But the insured managed to incorporate his drivers name as the person driving at the material time of accident in all documents, which the surveyor took no notice of. Not only the helper was driving at mid-night but also he was solely responsible for the accident since neither he had the skill nor the proper license.

For the reason best known to the surveyor, he overlooked this aspect, which was the most crucial and submitted his report accordingly. Although the insurance company rejected the claim, the scope of realising the claim through some other forum was not ruled out. Such unfortunate financial consequences could be avoided by being present at the site of accident to analyse pros and cons in the light of scope and exclusion of the policy.

Theft Impossible

One case that had defied all logic and reason in the world was a burglary claim. It was reported by the insured that his godown had been looted in the night of the super cyclone of 1999 and 950 tins of edible oil, each weighing 16 kg had been taken away. Responding to his FIR, the police gave their final report confirming the case was true but no clue. The concerned insurance officials performed the role of one of Gandhiji's proverbial monkeys that is to see no evil and thus the learned surveyor took the entire freedom of scrutinising insured's books of accounts and confirmed the genuineness and assessed the loss for Rs 6 lakh.

Now the question is when the godown was surrounded by four-feet of rainwater and the cyclonic storm was blowing at an unprecented speed of 265km per hour, even the bravest of men would dare not come out of their homes risking their life. In such circumstances in the darkness, especially when trees and electric poles were falling apart at quick succession how could anybody think of breaking open the shutters of a godown to steal nothing else but edible oil of such huge quantity? No doubt, the people deserved nothing less than the bravery award for confirming the impossible, which in any stretch of imagination was not possible but regrettably generated the scope for unpardonable leakage of public money.

Food for new thoughts

Today when loss of revenue is an annual feature, these are some of the ways to offset the lack-lustre performance by intelligently monitoring the survey activity. Unless inflated assessment is nipped in the bud, the clients may have the advantage of recovering that excess amount through various grievance redressal forums, since only the underwriters appoint the surveyors and not the insured. Therefore, we should train officers on the basics of engineering, on handling stock claims, its accounting intricacies, the detection of fraud, the avenues of checking inflated assessment and manipulation of documents. One doubts, if the huge spend on training includes such vital measures. If such prudent steps are taken with determination, the shock from the disaster of financial breakdown can be insulated.

Unless insurance officials are dead serious about it right now, it may be too late to recover. It gives enough food for new thinking as to how to overcome such stumbling blocks with which the industry is hugely affected. If private sector can do it, why not PSUs.? They should focus on these aspects through intense research, prudent analysis and constant training of officials.

It is the urgent need of present times that management of PSUs are required to revisit their decision on claim management plans and focus on minimisation strategies because it involves money and money is what matters.

CHAPTER 7

Tragic Tale of an Epic Claim

You cannot fool all of the people all the time.
— Abraham Lincoln

History repeats itself. The bad parts repeat more often than the good parts. But men do not learn anything from its repetition. The thirst for acquisition continues. The wealthiest man in the world wants more wealth. The most powerful seeks more power. All this despite knowing that the process of acquiring would amount to loss of god- given-peace-and-grace in life. An English proverb says, "Fools rush in where angels fear to tread." Temptation is one such area with an ever-inviting look. But it is like quicksand. If you take one step in, it will take you two steps down and finally into the bottomless pit. It often makes one so mad that one starts making every possible mistake and gets entangled in a cob-web of troubles. The irony is that the deceiver never knows how much he has deceived himself. It is like building safety houses made of matchboxes. This marine claim was of titanic proportions involving scuttling of two ships, two unscrupulous captains, a vagabond ship owner, a disgraced consignor and hundreds of people innocently aiding and abetting the crime of managing two shiploads of bogus cargo, freight forwarders fabricating reams of adulterated documents, thirty seven letters of credit defrauding eight reputed banks, conspirators pertaining to various countries like India, Singapore, China, Taiwan, Malaysia, Philippines and Thailand emitting the putrefying stench of conspiracy. Here goes the engrossing account of those tragic transactions.

The tragic flaw

V Kumar and R Kumar, two tycoons were the largest importers of palm oil mainly purchased from Bhatias of Singapore. It was in April 1976, driven by the strong desire to make easy money, Kumar Brothers involved Bhatias in a scheme whereby the latter would ship coconut oil to Kumars but which was to be declared in the ship's manifest as palm oil. This was so planned because coconut oil was a prohibited item for import into India, while palm oil was not. Accordingly, in September 1976 Bhatias dispatched the shipment. But the Kumars ran into trouble. However, being very influential, they knew that the Customs in Bombay had known. They edged out the Custom Authorities by diverting m.v. Her Majesty first to Karachi and then to Dubai where she anchored for a very long period, resulting in a huge demurrage bill. Eventually the vessel was ordered to sail to Penang where the coconut oil packed in drums was discharged into lighters and then brought down to Singapore where the consignment was transferred into bulk tanks and was sold to Motilal & sons. The 10,000 drums thus emptied were stored in Bhatia's warehouse. V Kumar fell victim to his own illegal activity and incurred a loss of US$ 2.5 million towards demurrage. He was deeply shaken but his temptation got up from its deep slumber with added strength. He decided to recover this loss by targeting insurance companies without realizing the chaos that it would unleash.

The plot

Sometime in March 1977 Kumar brothers flew to Singapore and met the Bhatias. They conspired to ship bogus cargoes in a vessel that was to be scuttled. The reasons to execute this scheme was to tide over the financial loss of that failed transaction of coconut oil.

V Kumar decided to have consignments consisting of 400 metric tons of metal scraps, 8000 metric tons of pvc resin, and balance bulk of clove and palm oil since no special licenses were required for their import into India. His own friend, SP Verma's group of companies would open letters of credit for these cargoes and to make things look genuine, would persuade his other clients in India to order for similar goods and to open letters of credit. On their part the Bhatias would use all their three firms Ovexpo, Buyexpo and Palmexpo Enterprises to act as the suppliers to prevent any suspicion from arising, should only one of their companies appear as the sole supplier. V Kumar wanted the Bhatias to do all the necessar y documentation that would normally be done by a shipper.

The booty of both V Kumar and SP Verma would be 50% of the total value of all the letters of credit received and negotiated by Bhatia's companies. This sum was to be remitted by Bhatia to them by post- dated cheques drawn on his bank accounts which would be honoured as and when funds were credited into those accounts from the proceeds of negotiated letters of credit.

The remaining 50% would be disbursed for the expenses which would include the purchase of ship, payments for freight bills and to the authors of false documents to be used and other expenses like port charges, transport charges, purchase of wooden crates, bags and renting of warehouses. It was envisaged that the Bhatias too would benefit about 20% from this balance 50%.

The cargo would be shipped on C & F basis. The insurance of the fake cargo and the eventual claims, would be the sole responsibility of V Kumar mainly because of his considerable influence in that field. Bhatia tightened his jaws while accepting this complex assignment and was left racking his brain on how to execute this nefarious design. But finally he was drawn in to the vortex. With this, his mind migrated from business activity to subversive activity and he became a willing participant in the scheme. Little did he realize that this would land him in murky waters. The Bhatias contacted Peter Lay (the ship owner with a notorious past record of scuttling ships) to sound him out on the proposed scheme. He wanted US$ 2 million to execute a perfect script for scuttling a vessel. Peter, a-fly-by night operator, on persuasion agreed for US$ 1.5 million. It was an explosion of opportunity for him to use one of his own rust buckets M. V. Caverilla in the scheme, the repair of which was overdue and over expensive. It was agreed that the fee would cover one vessel with a load of 7,000 tons of cargo. As if enough is not enough, with inner agitation and irresistible anxiety V Kumar gave an unexpected and thrilling twist to the plot. He wanted a second vessel. This was because the total cargo ordered by buyers, far exceeded 7000 tons that m. v. Caverilla could carry.

As the letters of credit for the excess cargo had already been established, Kumar was worried that it might have adverse effect in implementing the scheme. He therefore asked for another vessel for that purpose. Peter looked frightened and was reluctant. Bhatias were equally apprehensive. However, conquered by V Kumar's enthusiasm, Peter who had the habit of flirting with danger got geared up to sacrifice another vessel for a similar fee.

The first sting

The m. v. Caverilla arrived in Singapore in July 1977 Peter met Sucharto, the Chief Engineer and persuaded to assist him in scuttling the vessel on her next voyage as he had done in scuttling m. v. Karenina in the past. But this was the very reason why Sucharto refused to do the dirty job and soil his dignity again. He was, however, promised a lucrative sum of US$ 45,000 and finally he succumbed to the temptation. Peter then outlined his plan, which was to cut holes in the bulkheads between the different holds of the vessel so that when water was let into the engine room through the sea-valves, the flooding within the vessel will be quicker. For this operation they used the services of Lao Lee the proprietor of Sun Light Engineering and the job was done.

In August 1977, Peter informed Lao Lee of the arrival

of m. v. oh Kai. As instructed Lee unleashed a dose of pure cruelty by cutting seven holes through the bulkheads separating the engine room from the first hold, the first hold from the second and the second from the third and so on. These holes were then covered with metal plates and temporarily screwed as if the ship was stabbed in her stomach and was operated upon with temporary stitches.

Forged documents on metal scrap

Bhatia was the dictator of the scheme. He bossed everybody around. Thus Ronaldo the smart director of Victor Pvt Ltd dealing in metal scrap did a cameo for Bhatia. He agreed to give him relevant documents relating to the fake supply of scrap. Bhatia gave him necessary details to prepare the proforma invoices, packing lists and fictitious correspondence in proof of the supply of metal scrap to the companies of Bhatias. With documents ready, Ronaldo approached Alvin Lim of Rumy Metals, to supply him with corresponding invoices and packing lists to evidence in turn the supply of same material to his company. This was intended to support Ronaldo's so called supply of the same scrap to the Bhatias. Alvin Lim was promised by Ronaldo a payment of one percent of the invoiced value. He obliged and got the reward in return.

Plot on PVC resin and Clove

Bhatia had a museum of ideas inside his skull. He apprised Jackson that he had a large consignment of pvc resin and clove to be shipped to India but was in difficulties as the terms in the letters of credit stipulated that the shipper could not be both the supplier and manufacturer of the commodities. He therefore wanted Jackson's assistance to provide him with sales documents from Newhouse International Ltd for clove and from Apex Exim Ltd for pvc resin. Jackson's deputy, Swaminathan understood correctly that their two companies would be issuing documents to the Bhatias showing the sale of clove and pvc resin without supplying the same. Bhatia told that for this service, their two companies would benefit financially from him. A docile Swaminathan showed the least sign of resistance and agreed.

All the documents for the sale of clove and pvc resin to Bhatia's companies were prepared and signed by Swaminathan. Bhatia blessed the transaction by giving US$ 0.2 million to Swaminathan for his role in the scheme. He too collected similar documents of US$ 7.7 million worth for the fake sale of resin from quality plastics to his company through Apex Exim in similar manner.

The Bhatias purchased a small quantity of clove and kept in their warehouse so that the aroma of that spice would induce his own staff to assume that he was actually dealing in clove. His staff prepared outward delivery orders for clove that the Bhatias were purpor ting to ship to India. The consignment of clove that Newhouse was to deliver to m. v. Caverilla was, incidentally, the purported "clove" that Haridas Nair had already packed in bags with rice bran extraction.

Cooked up bank transactions

To authenticate the fake supply of cargo in question a complex system of payments to suppliers was devised. Cheques were made in favour of Newhouse, Apex, Rumy Metals and Ban Kee under an arrangement whereby the sums so paid would be refunded in cash. As regards the payments to Newhouse and Apex, the Bhatias had opened bank accounts in the name of these two companies with the Tao Lee bank. He got several cheque books issued under these accounts pre-signed by Swaminathan. Eventually, cheques drawn by Bhatia were deposited into the accounts of Apex and Newhouse, operated by Swaminathan. An examination of the statements of accounts of both Apex and Newhouse, when were compared with that of Ovexpo, revealed that large amounts of money appear to have been deposited and withdrawn by using cheques pre-signed by Swaminathan giving the impression of a very active business relationship between the companies in question.

The palm oil plot

Following his agreement with Bhatias, Charlie Hua, owner of Ban Kee, provided forged documents to evidence the the supply about 5,000 metric tons of palm oil to Ovexpo for US$ 5 million. Charlie got US$ 0.24 million as cash award for his role in the scheme.

Rice barn for resin

Swaminathan placed an order for 21,000 kraft paper bags with Pape products Pvt Ltd and filled each of them with 25 kg rice barn extraction. When 1000 wooden cases arrived, he had them stuffed with the rice barn filled paper bags. This job was done at breathless pace. Of the 1,000 wooden cases so prepared for shipment only 500 of them were marked for the m.v. Caverilla. Swaminathan transported these cases to wharves arranged for their loading. The remaining 500 cases were taken to m.v. oh. Kai in last week of August.

The Herculean task

In July 1977 Bhatia instructed Nair to prepare part of the palm oil consignment as palletized items.

Hence, Nair purchased about 8,000 empty biscuit tins and 8,000 cardboard cartoons and 200 pallets from various sources. He had the empty biscuit tins filled with water, which was mixed with saffron to give a yellowish tinge to it for passing off as palm oil. The filled tins were then packed into the cardboard cartons and stacked onto the pallets to await their transport to the vessels. In addition to false transport bills that were issued by Instant Freight Forwarders, Haridas Nair, the marine surveyor issued certificates of quality, quantity, analysis and weight in respect of palm oil, clove, pvc resin and metal scraps. These documents were required to negotiate letters of credit with the concerned banks.

Loading in the vessel

On 8 August 77, while loading in m.v. Caverilla was in progress, Haridas Nair received a message that capt. Joseph, an insurance investigator from India was trying to contact him. Later Bhatia contacted Nair for an immediate meeting as capt. Joseph had inquired about the loading details for the clove shipment. Bhatia, Nair, and Lim Song Hua decided that the clove for the next vessel be loaded at Boat Quay as this was a long stretch and there were no fixed loading points alongside. Boat Quay was also selected because it would prevent capt. Joseph from making any surprise checks on the shipment of clove. This was how Mr. Bhatia's so called precious cargoes did the hop, step and the final jump into the vessels.

Macabre Acts of Scuttling

The m. v. Caverilla started on 11 August 1977, sailed for six days before Capt. Brute stopped the engines and idled the vessel in the sea for three weeks. After receiving a coded message from Peter on 3 September 1977, he positioned the vessel in deep sea and in the morning next after dispatching the crew in lifeboats, instructed the chief engineer to open the sea valves. The metal plates over the holes cut into bulkheads had been removed earlier. The Captain, and the Chief Engineer waited until the engine room was sufficiently flooded before taking a life-boat to safety. The sea was relaxed and when the aluminum glow of dawn was descending from heaven, the ship sank with a heavy heart. The sky which was bright and blue got blackened in the next moment. The morning star closed its eyes with shame and disappeared. The star will come again but the ship will never. The master of the ship became a slave of temptation and did not hesitate to destroy something, which he was supposed to protect. Only four days after the tragedy of m. v. Caverilla when the underwriters got the news of m. v. oh Kai sinking on 7 September 1977 off the coast of Myanmar under similar circumstances. Jaws dropped, eyebrows raised and underwriters sniffed something fishy. Capt. Prathap and the chief engineer Baadman supervised the removal of the iron plates. As soon as the engine room was flooded, the ship, quietly cried before being choked by death. Her appeal for mercy was unheard to the cruel Captain. Rightly the underwriters suspected a foul play and the story spread instantly among the insurance circles, provided gossip fodder and nutrified the rumour-mill as it went from office to office.

Quantum of the Sin

In August 1977 the Bhatias had submitted thirty-seven letters of credit, each with a set of bill of exchange, the invoice and the bill of lading, the respective packing lists, weight and quality certificates, supplier's certificates, certificates of dispatch, certificates of origin and cable advice to various banks in Singapore for negotiations. All these documents represented the cargo that never existed. Twenty five transactions were successfully concluded and the banks involved did pay the amounts in question into the respective accounts of Ovexpo, Buyexpo and Palmexpo.

The Investigation

Two ships sinking in quick succession, carrying the

cargo of same people, sailing from the same port, to the same destination from the same consignors was tell-tale symptom for captain Joseph to suspect and read through the game. It is common knowledge that ships do not sink on calm waters. It was believed that the vessels Caverilla did not carry any hull insurance whereas in case of oh Kai, the hull underwriters had repudiated their liability on a claim made by the ship owners. From the documents furnished by the various claimants it had become evident that in many cases, the goods had been shipped and the bills of lading were issued even before the respective ships arrived. Cloves were not cultivated in Singapore and the total quantity of clove imported to that country during the whole year was much less than the quantity shipped in this case. It came to light that Jackson the high profile Director of Newhouse International had been arrested in connection with the sinking of Ocean Glory wherein the said company was alleged to have consigned certain purported goods. He was also charged for cheating a foreign bank by using false shipping documents worth of US$ 1.3 million and had been convicted for that.

On behalf of the underwriters captain Joseph lodged a complaint with the commercial crime division, stating that there were reasonable grounds to suspect that the vessels had been scuttled. It was not a big challenge for Singapore police to get to the bottom of fraud and nail the truth because the accused had admitted to their crimes under harsh interrogation. The police started a flurry of probes against Bhatias, Jackson and Swaminathan and it was difficult for the accused to wriggle out of the long arms of the law.

The Arrests

Criminal proceedings were initiated in Singapore on the evidence that the real cargo was not shipped. Swaminathan was arrested on 26 January 1981 together with Jackson, who had already been serving sentence for scuttling m. v. Ocean Glory. Ronaldo was sent to jail on 28 January 1981.In the afternoon on 16 April 1981 the tainted Bhatia and cunning Peter were arrested.

The Tragic Fall

In August 1981 Bhatia was sentenced to four years in jail. He found it impossible to wriggle out of this pit unharmed. With the bliss of his sleep gone he lost his appetite for food, sank deeply into solitude measuring and re-measuring the depth of misfortune that his misdeeds had brought to his otherwise comfortable life. Meeting even his dear ones became an annoyance. Burning with repentance, he kept weeping day in and day out over his unfortunate fate. He was often seen lying on the solitary bed curled up like a dead shrimp. The unbearable thought of his rotten act floated endlessly in the guilty corner of his mind. He was ostracized as a fraudster. He paced up and down in jail room searching for a remedy that could redeem his past. A man among men, six-foot tall, broad-shouldered with punishing forearms got reduced to a bagful of bones chewing on his quiet penance. The ghost of his past tightened the noose into strangling grip around his soul and sucked the life-blood out of him. He was barely recognizable and with sunken eyes he looked like the abstract idea of a human form. The jail room had a funeral echoes. The thought that his life had been written off frightened him. Finally his restless heart stopped throbbing to bring an end to all his miseries. The catharsis happened.It silenced all the noise inside his head. The tragic end came during trial. That was how he paid a heart-breaking price for his extraordinary stupidity.

Jackson got four years concurrently with eleven years he was then facing in connection with the scuttling of another vessel and Swaminathan was awarded 18 months. Peter had the company of terrible solitude in the jail. He was granted bail on a US$ 3 million bond, jumped bail and finally fled to Puerto Rico and walked into the sunset and sank below the horizon.

Verma, unable to cope with the ominous consequences, died of a massive heart attack. The importers in India were at loggerheads with the underwriters to recover money under the insurance policies issued to them for covering various consignments which were never shipped. Decades passed. Arguments and counter arguments continued making the conclusion difficult to arrive.

Lessons learnt

In Marine trade, many times one has to underwrite without seeing the subject matter of insurance. Hence it is a risky business and requires a high degree of experience, know-how and imagination. It is therefore pertinent for the marine underwriter to be alert and maintain detailed and informative statistics per commodity, per client, per country of origin and the ship owner. All these however should be supported by the application of his intuition.

In the present case such huge consignments worth millions of dollars should have been pre-inspected. Cloves, pvc resins and metal scrap were not part of the regular business of the Kumars. Underwriters should have sniffed the foul play. Two vessels with Panama flags, belonging to Peter Lay, a shady character whose assets were those two vessels only and who has been known to have had his ships sunk in the past, were more hazardous risks than vessels belonging to well known shipping companies with good record and reputation. Moral hazards are many times more dangerous than accidental hazards. After going all the way to Singapore, Captain Joseph should have inspected the cargoes. No one knows what hijacked his attention. The seaworthiness of the vessels should have been looked into before accepting so much of risk in the said vessels. Such proposals must have been referred to the central office of the underwriters. They could have suggested taking precautionary measures. One may say that it is easy to be wiser after the event but undoubtedly it would provide an insight to the future underwriters of the world that flash point in marine underwriting too is very low.

Gentle Reminder

The Kumars committed a blunder in coconut oil conspiracy but learnt nothing despite paying a heavy price. But again they befriended the Bhatias in committing a greater blunder in scuttling two vessels which made their otherwise luxurious life, a tragedy of discomfort and thereby contributed an ugly chapter to marine insurance history for all time to come. This ghastly episode will stand out as a lighthouse cautioning the underwriters the rock of fraud that could be hidden under the apparently smooth waters of marine proposal. Now one understands what great Warren Buffet has said 'Insurance is a financial weapon of mass destruction'. Hence let's never underestimate the intelligence of the manipulators.

Capt.Joseph who was appointed for pre-despatch inspection of the said consignments by the underwriters , saw the loading from a distance and gave a clean report. Had he opened one drum and seen the contents of water inside, the story would have been different. If a responsible officer from the Insurance Company would have accompanied him, the whole mess would have been prevented.If the underwriters would have filed a suit against the negligent surveyors, a lesson would have been learnt for those with lackadaisical approach to their duty.Even after four decades the case was in the court. What a mess my Lord !

CHAPTER 8

Underwriting Controversial Risks

Intellectuals solve problems; geniuses prevent them.

Einstein

General Insurance claims are no stranger to controversies and that is why those are vulnerable to get trapped in the legal loop. Ultimately purpose of prudent underwriting is judicious and peaceful settlement of claims and prevention economic turmoil. It is more needed especially when claim ratio diagram is going through the roof. Thus the underwriters should add extra spring to their steps to rise to the occasion and sharpen their underwriting skills.

Sudden increase in sum insured: read between the lines

Let us take some flashes from our past claim experiences. A certain stock was insured for Rs 40 lakh. Three months later, the insured got it enhanced to Rs 1 crore. Again three months after the same stock insurance was increased to Rs 2 crore. Two months thereafter the factory under mysterious circumstances was gutted by a huge fire .The stock alone was assessed for Rs.1.6 crore apart from building, plant and machinery. Since the insured had availed loan from the bank, his cash flow statement was examined by the underwriters and it was found that purchase of raw materials during months preceding fire was only to the tune of Rs 16 lakh and the sale of finished products was to the extent of Rs 17 lakh per month. The controversy refused to die with discovery of more fraudulent documents and the problem remained unresolved for a decade. Finally, the decision went in favour of the insured.

A little application of intelligence by the underwriting office at the time of increasing the sum insured twice by such exorbitant amount could have avoided such bitter controversy that claimed huge amount of legal fees on both sides because as the proverb says lawyers and woodpeckers have long bills. Since it was a processing unit, how could the insured increase his stock by five times without corresponding increase in plant and machinery. Of course asking for bank statement at the time of such unusual increase in sum insured would have been insightfully intuitive. It is high time therefore, the underwriters make underwriting of controversial risks their sole focus-point especially at a time when companies' balance sheets are bleeding profusely because of avoidable claims.

Generators: generating trouble on reinstatement

Three generator sets of Yamaha make were insured for Rs 1.3 crore on reinstatement value basis under standard fire and special perils policy. Prior to acceptance of the proposal the risk was inspected by an engineer. Five months after the commencement of the cover, the insured property got damaged by fire. The surveyor submitted his report without a semblance of exactitude because he assumed the reinstatement value of damaged property as Rs 10 crore. Since the sum insured was only Rs 1.30 crore the net liability of the underwriters was arrived at Rs 1.30 crore. But the learned surveyor charged his survey fees on the assessment of Rs 10 crore. and produced invoices of new three Yamaha gen.sets of same make in support thereof.

The underwriters asked for the original purchase invoices of the gen-sets which the insured could not produce. An investigator was appointed. It was found that the survey report was a pale reflection of truth because these generators were twenty five years old and were purchased from the ship breaking yard on weight basis for a sum of Rs 40 lakh. Hence it was but natural that purchase invoice could not be available. The claim naturally got pole-vaulted into controversy.

The surveyor argued in favour of settling the claim for Rs 1.3 crore citing the basis of valuation as present day replacement value i.e Rs 10 crore less depreciation for number of years used. When referred to the experts, it was confirmed that although it was insured on reinstatement value basis, the final indemnity would be donkey for the donkey and not horse for the donkey. Hence only Rs 40 lakh would be payable. The surveyor should therefore scale down his assessment but he was adamant sticking to his gun. The claim was referred to the special committee of the Institute of Sur veyors. The special committee opined that the liability of the underwriters would be Rs 40 lakhs being the actual price paid for the three gen-sets. The insured filed a case in Consumer Forum for Rs 1.30 crore and after scrutinizing all the documents the hon'ble forum directed the insurance company to deposit Rs 40 lakh.

When asked why did he give a favourable pre-inspection and valuation report for Rs 1.30 crore, the pre-inspection engineer spun out an unconvincing explanation saying that it was because the party wanted the report for the sake of availing a bank loan. Some insurance pundits argue that insured is entitled for market value of gen-sets irrespective of the fact that he had obtained the same by dubious means. They say that if the insured had obtained the machinery as dowry, would not he be entitled to the market value? They also argue that law has made an allowance for the wrong things to get a chance and unless amended otherwise, the surveyor is entitled to his fees on reinstatement value assessment of losses as per present guidelines.

With claim ratio increasing fast and furious, meritorious underwriting is a must before accepting very old machinery for insurance on reinstatement value basis under fire policy. It is because in case the insured succumbs to the temptation of arson, it is very difficult to bring that to light and he can get away with huge profit if he insures such machinery on reinstatement value basis. Should we not avoid insuring machinery more than five years old on reinstatement value basis of the insured whose moral sease is not above suspicion. All that the underwriter need to do is to assess, analyze and act accordingly..

Trouble with the double covers

When stocks held in trust are insured both by the owners and the processing unit, calculation of indemnity becomes a Herculean task. For example, Ratan Kumar had taken fire insurance policy from a PSU company for Rs 12 crore covering stock-held in trust in his cloth processing unit. He was charging the merchants a certain amount of money for processing and dyeing their grey clothes. Everything was going on well until a fire broke out on the ground and first floor of his four storeyed factory premises. The insured submitted a big list of 108 merchants whose stocks were lying in the factory premises at the time of fire. The situation became complicated when 28 of these merchants had insured their stock with different underwriters and claimed separately. The matter came to light when 28 different surveyors representing respective underwriters arrived at the site for survey and what followed was a domino effect of problems.

- The problem of underwriters of 28 customers asking for contribution from the stock-held-in-trust insurer.
- What would be the basis of contribution? Since processing house (insured) has not taken customer-wise insurance.
- The segregation of the saved stock customer wise and valuation of salvage thereof.
- The total coinsurance share might exceed the total sum insured of the main underwriter.

To avoid all such complicated issues it should clearly be mentioned in the policy that this insurance does not cover that stock in cases where insurance has already been taken by the owners of the stock separately. A little care at the time of underwriting will prevent all complications of coinsurance apportionment at the time of claim. Upper level of stock holding period must also be fixed in the policy itself. For example if the stocks have been lying for more than six months, the policy will not respond for any claim in respect of such claim.

Floater policy that can become a whirlpool for the underwriters

A fire floater policy was issued covering 400 godowns. A huge fire damaged three of those insured godowns. The insured claimed 90% of the total sum insured for the loss of stock in these godowns reporting that the rest of the godowns barring one were empty. This gave rise to tremendous technical headache for the underwriters because it was not possible to check the saved stock in the rest of 397 godowns. Only on the basis of volumetric measurement and verification of salvage, the turbulent claim amount got subsided to 25% of the sum insured. Such incidences scarcely show our underwriters with glory.

Apart from many underwriting precautions, it should be mandatory to fix maximum limit of sum insured per locations in terms of certain percentage of the total sum insured. This little application will prevent lots of problems at the time of claim. Care should also be taken to avoid giving floater policy to cover those godowns which keep stocks with multiple ownership. Identification of stock after fire in such cases becomes hassle-ridden affair. What is underwritten and how it is underwritten decide the quality of claim settlement especially now when the balance sheets of insurance companies are not in the pink of their health. The writing on the wall is loud and clear and they must learn their lessons right. If they do not do learn it today, tomorrow may be too late and those who do not learn from history are condemned to repeat it.

CHAPTER 9

Beauty of Weather Insurance

Wherever you go, no matter what the weather, always bring your own sunshine.

Sunshine is delicious, rain is refreshing and snow is exciting. There is no such thing as bad weather. But a definite quality and quantity of sunshine and rain are required for the seeds to germinate, blossom forth and be productive to the fullness of their potentiality. Down the ages more often than not, weather has not been dependable in this respect. Hence insurable. Weather underwriters assess the deficit in crop output due to adverse weather incidents with the help of statistical methods and crop modeling. They analyse computerized data-base loaded with 30 years of weather statistics to estimate the probability of loss- causing weather occurrences. Then they set out an objective parameter such as level of rainfall requirement at a specific location for a specific crop during an agreed period. Rain does not come according to the estimate of statistics. Like weather it comes in its unpredictable measure of either more or less. Hence claims. The term sheets which form the basis of the contract correlate weather fluctuation as accurately as possible with loss of agriculture production suffered by farmers. The financial loss of the insured farmer is estimated on the basis of deviation from agreed weather conditions and payouts are delivered without delay. Like proper ty insurance it never pretends to be more than what it is—neither exhibiting its wide scope nor concealing the implosive exclusions.

All the insured farmers within the same area receive payouts on the basis of weather abnormality experienced at reference weather station installed in their area and mentioned in the contract thereby eliminating the need of expensive, time consuming, subjective and lengthy crop cutting method of loss assessment. What matters is not only how much you pay but how quickly you pay what you pay.

Heart of the subject matter

The payouts may not always co-relate with the loss of

production suffered by the farmer. There is reason to be skeptical on certain fronts. For example inspired by the adverse weather forecast an insured farmer may not cultivate but will take away a claim if the weather goes bad and is recorded so. A big farmer in possession of huge stretch of barren land will grab this opportunity and can go all out for weather insurance with unstoppable enthusiasm because about 75% of actuarial premium is patronized by the Government and what he pays is affordable for the poor. Some wise farmers may irrigate their land and have the full harvest and yet can get benefit under deficit rainfall insurance. With the drip irrigation in place, a farmer can scientifically utilize limited availability of water and yet can get both the claim and the desired yield.

In another spectrum of the possibility, there is a chance that some farmers can take deficit rainfall insurance but instead of cultivating crop A which needs more water they can cultivate crop B which needs less water and can have both the claim in case of deficit rainfall and adequate harvest of his crop as well.

Payouts: Simplifying indemnity

The orthodox insurance scholars may scream out questions that the principle of insurable interest which is so vital in property and liability insurance is less remembered and the least emphasized. But this type of insurance is done on good faith and not on utmost good faith. Therefore a little violation of the rigid principle of insurance does not influence the settlement of claim. Since the risk units are very small and locations being very far and inaccessible, it will not be cost effective to check the bits and pieces.

It doesn't follow the principle of indemnity either, since it is index based insurance, uniform indemnity is given to all farmers in the particular area despite dissimilar losses. Thus it is collective indemnity and weather is used as a proxy to the yield index and payouts are not on the basis of assessing the actual losses. Too much of law is unlawful for the comforts of man. Therefore it is no harm calling it benefit insurance and not insurance of indemnity.

In property insurance customer relationship disintegrates in commitment- deficit scenario. But here claim payouts are machine made, not as perceived by man and influenced by his personal opinion but as received by the dispassionate machine and therefore has little scope for subjective assessment. In fact, the payouts are arithmetically agreed upon at the time of underwriting. How beautiful and how hassle free! The weather underwriting industry which is dedicated to insuring against nature's unpredictable moods also benefits from the design of the coverage it grants because if it pays under excess rainfall, it doesn't have to pay under deficit rainfall and vice-versa although premium is collected for both. In case both the contra-dictory covers are opted, a discount in premium will be a rational decision. It is very unlikely scenerio that opposite events would happen simultaneously in the very same place.

Weather Station: the mechanical judge

Seated like a mechanical judge, automatic weather station is tasked with recording the atmospheric variables like humidity, temperature and rainfall. It works with clinical precision because it has the final say in deciding the payouts, thereby making the whole insurance transaction quite transparent. It can sometimes be vulnerable and be influenced in which case the claim can change sides, the details of which need not be elaborated for security reasons. But weather station system is accessorized with additional software for checking the data in case it is tampered with. For example with variation in actual rainfall, the temperature and humidity will accordingly vary. If only rainfall activity is manipulated, the other two unaltered data will expose it and raise an alarm for the underwriters to take corrective measures. It is not possible to tamper with all the systems proportionately and simultaneously.

Moreover, it is okay in matters of humidity and temperature but the rain is not always ubiquitous. It appears unannounced and disappears quietly. It may rain at one end of the village and may not rain at the other end at the same time. But the whole insured area has to share the fortune and the misfortune of the tiny spot where the automatic weather station is located and not on the basis of the weather deviations suffered in the insured's field. It amounts to be part determining the whole which more often may not reflect the actual experienced reality of rainfall of each insured field. Making indemnity available in absolutely right measures to each individual farmer in India is an insurmountable hurdle because of small land holdings in huge numbers. Despite little bits of anomalies here and there, weather insurance is considered as the most preferred option for the farmers in India.

The back-up station: ensuring the insurance

Weather station is right at the heart of the scheme. If the heartbeat stops, the operation of the scheme will stop. Therefore, a back-up weather station and sometimes back-up to the back-up is necessary. If weather station A falls sick and does not do its duty, the insured farmers are entitled to either compensation or no compensation as per the reading of the neighboring weather station B which is called back up weather station. But it may so happen that weather condition under A is absolutely normal and weather condition under B absolutely abnormal. In such a case the farmers under A will have two harvests: one from cultivation and the other from claim compensation. The situation could be just the opposite as well, that is, he may neither get the crop nor the claim. But such stray situations are very rare and have to be overlooked in a huge operation and in the greater interest of the farmer community.

The excluded peril : Time to think

If there is cloudburst on distant mountain slopes and such water flows flooding the un-rained insured fields thereby suffocating the crops and hopes of the farmers, the weather station has no intelligence to record such havoc. Hence, disappointingly no payouts are made at the time of such disaster. Man has to think hard for the machine to include this aspect.

Mission possible:Insulating the future shock

Scientists have given a feverish statement that the global temperature has gone up by 0.74 degree celsius during last 100 years. The 10 warmest years globally since 1880 have shockingly descended on earth during last 13 years. Because of the infidelity committed by chemical industries, smelter plants and coal consuming power plants by emitting unbearable heat and obscene quantity of suffocating materials, mother nature is in no mood to be calm and kind. Under such circumstances weather insurance is a life saving device for poor farmers. It can compensate them against the wrath of the weather and can reduce their financial worries, generate income for the broker and can take the footprints of the crop insurance industry into places where roads have not gone and civilization has made but a little impression.

Battling odd is nothing new to the poor farmers of our country but it is good to see them smiling and looking optimistic. His share of mere two and half percent premium is an offer no farmers can afford to refuse because having paid, adverse weather can no more spell doom in their lives. They no longer have to look heavenwards in despair. There is some poetic flavour in this insurance device that softly, echoes Shelley's famous lines, 'If winter comes, can spring be far behind ?'

CHAPTER 10

Painful Compensation: TP Claims

"What you do not want done to yourself, do not do to others"
Confucius

No law is sufficiently convenient to all. Motor third party cases are not the cases of crime and punishment, those are simply not be and thus need compensation matters of payment of referred to the cumbersome, time consuming and expensive process of motor accident claims tribunal for settlement. Why should someone, who is already in terrible distress, has to be forced to pay the lawyer's fees at times to the tune of 40% of the award amount for getting his or her rightful payment? It is a deplorable irony that two parties that are mainly the insurance companies on one hand and the victims or their legal heirs in case of death on the other that are pulled into the gruesome legal battle without any dispute arising between them and only because a system exists and the system is too complicated to be useful for the people concerned.

Endless waiting

For example on 12 August 1991 our cricket hero Chandrasekhar was crippled by a cruel motor accident, a truck crushing his left leg. It was from the hospital bed that he filed a petition on 11 January 1992 for compensation. Although 14-long painful years of his disabled life had passed, he was yet to get his much needed compensation. He could neither sit nor move without stress and strain. Chandrasekhar's case is not an isolated example. There are more than one million cases pending in various MACTs of the country. If we take three dependants in each case more than three million desperate people are waiting for their rightful payment for years and some of them will have to wait for decades as in the case of Chandrasekhar.

The huge Sum

The huge amount of about Rs 12,000 crore that is being parked in the insurance companies' investment accounts is the money that belongs to the 10 lakh families of the poor and destitute which constitute about 30- lakhs dependants who are leading broken lives because someone very dear in their family has died or has been maimed in the cruel road accident. It is the money that is needed to buy medicine for the sick, food for the hungry and education for the deprived. When we create earthquakes in case of delay in the payment of our salary, let us put ourselves in their shoes and walk a mile to know how it feels to wait for years with tears not drying up in the eyes. This problem is worse than Orissa cyclone, Gujarat earthquake and recent tsunami put together. It is because the victims are scattered all over the country, its magnitude goes unnoticed. The disposal ratio in the existing system is 21% which means without admitting new cases (which is as high as 27%), it will take more than five years to clear the backlog and cases admitted now will have to wait five long years to have its turn for disposal.

In Saudi Arab if a motor vehicle hits a man fatally on the road, the driver remains behind the bar until the compensation amount which is called diya or the blood money is paid to the legal heir of the deceased which is 1.5 lakh rials for the Muslim male, 0.75 lakh rials for the Christian male and 0.375 lakh for others. Women and children get 50% of the respective amounts. It does not take more than a week for the matter to be sorted out by the police.

The Alternative

Time is ripe enough for the law makers of the country to sit up and take notice of the fact that justice can be delivered fast not by complicating law and its procedure but by simplifying it especially when most of our country folks are ignorant of law. Thus the parliament should take it on priority to pass a bill to empower respective insurance companies to pay such claims the way they settle vehicle damage-claims which are of more complicated nature and are settled in about three months time and in which case settlement ratio is more than 80% and only few pending claims are more than one year old. Moreover the insurance companies are having more than 6,000 strong offices in every nook and corner of the country and to get claims paid from the nearest office will be a great advantage for the parties concerned. As per a write up in The Times of India by the former CVC N Vittal, thirty million cases are pending in various courts in our country. If the courts were to stop registering new cases and start disposing the pending cases only, it may take 100 years for all cases as of today to see the light of judgement. If such is the reality, the judiciary can divert the manpower from MACT to decide such more important cases and leaving T.P. cases to insurance companies.

Softening of law

The strength of law lies not in law books but in its coming out of those printed words and punishing the guilty so that it remains as a glaring example for people not to repeat such crimes in future. But punishment to unlicensed drivers causing fatal accidents is very rarely seen and compensation against such vehicle owners have not ever been awarded. Thus with no lessons learnt, irresponsible vehicle owners are encouraged to commit such illegal act of killing more and more people on the road every year by appointing drivers without license and continuing the services of the drunken drivers. With the length and breadth of the road remaining the same, with negligible number of driving schools in the country, with vehicle population rising by 20% every year, with more and more number of helpers at the wheels of loaded vehicles after midnight, trying to learn driving in heavy traffics, the rate of accident is most certainly going to accelerate alarmingly in such climates. With infrastructure of **MACT** remaining constant and with its complicated procedure remaining unaltered,it will not be able to cope up with this sky rocketing trend of accident cases that are and will be filed in large scale.

The rude reality check

Since the MACT neither punishes the unlicensed driver nor does it pass award against the owner of the vehicle appointing such drivers, what remains to be done in most of the cases is mere calculation of compensation. If the insurance companies will be authorised to settle these cases like vehicle damage claims, the delay will be reduced to the maximum extent, unnecessary paper work involving written statements and counters will be abolished, insurance company official will remain accountable for settlement thus the hundreds of bogus claims (according to newspaper sources) that are filed in various courts will not find their place with this kind of arrangement and the beneficiaries will get their full amount of award without giving a lion's share to the lawyers. For such an arrangement the payment of compensation should be more clearly structured by the law-makers without any ambiguity. With the non-licensed going scot-free, people are not interested to learn driving in driving schools, and vehicle owners are more and more careless in appointing such drivers whose driving of vehicles is no less dangerous than missiles on the road, ready to kill at any moment. When insurance companies are directed to pay even when the driver is at fault and the owner appointing such driver is at fault, there is nothing left to be analysed and judged for which cases keep waiting for years. Thus insurance companies should permanently be empowered to directly pay in such cases and recover the same amount from the guilty vehicle owners by filing recovery suits against them thus avoiding to fight the same case twice in the court. Thus the system of MACT which was designed to become a bridge between the beneficiaries and the insurance companies is standing like a wall between them by delaying a simple transaction of compensation to the helpless and the deprived. Any system that generates inordinate delay in giving the rightful compensation to the needy is not desirable and should be replaced by another system that could facilitate quick transaction. Hence the transfer of cases to the insurance companies is the crying need of these destitute millions and should be implemented right away without second thoughts.

CHAPTER 11

Countering man-made Claims

*Every mind is a genius. There are no other
kinds of mind in the world.*

- Osho

More than hundred percent combined ratio amounts to operational bankruptcy. Sizeable contribution to this sorry state of affair comes from man-made claims which have been a thorny issue pressing for urgent attention. These claims are thrill-inducing, mind-blowing and need to be tackled with extra intelligence. We must add spring to our steps to arrest alarming claim ratio. While we circle out pressing appointments on our daily calendar, instant visit to the site of claim should be given top priority to see the truth in its simplicity.

Coats on Fire

It happened in the western world. A claim management team visited the departmental store alleged to have huge stock of 3000 expensive coats destroyed by fire. The insured showed them the debris where coats were stored. In course of discussion the team leader asked him the specification of the coats. The insured told that they were made of high quality woolen fabrics with nine steel buttons in each coat that were three buttons at the end of each sleeve and three others to close the opening. The intuitive team being the master of their craft, calculated for a while and asked, 'Please show us the salvage of those melted 27000 steel buttons'. Steel stuff could certainly not evaporate with this sort of temperature.

This pointed question was like setting a cat among the pigeons. The insured was speechless because not a single melted button was there in the debris. He was trying to pull the wool over the eyes of the underwriters. He was embarrassed by the inconvenient truth. This knack of finding absolutely fresh insight lies in visiting the site of claims. It was later revealed that the stocks were removed before the store was set on fire. The insured at last decided to put a lid on the episode by withdrawing the claim.

Rusted bullets and polished settlement

An imported consignment of cartridges for bofors gun was insured for US$ 10 million. On arrival, rust damage of the whole consignment due to sea water was reported. If these rusted cartridges were used, it would backfire with reverse thrust because of the rust, hence considered total loss. The underwriters contacted a retired army Colonel, a brave Sikh who had a masterful knowledge of this type of gun. After a thorough investigation he confirmed that the rust could be removed and cartridges could be re-used. As a matter of demonstration, he removed the rust from the cartridge by using sand paper and himself test-fired successfully. The 16 Kg bullet zoomed into the sky aiming at nothing in particular dispelling the doubt of the army.

After a brief persuasion the clients agreed to remove rust from the cartridges and only the labour cost amounting to US$20,000 was paid and equal amount was paid to the retired army official as specialist fees thereby reducing the claim amount from US$ 10 million of total loss to just US$ 40,000. The claim on war items was peacefully settled. When insurance companies are in the choking grip of underwriting losses, such claim management tactics should not be consigned to the dustbins of complacency.

Same survey: two contradictory reports

Life-saving bulk drug was imported by a government pharmaceutical firm for capsule preparation. The consignment was insured by the suppliers up to Mumbai airport with overseas underwriters and a tail-end cover from Mumbai to the factory in Bangalore was arranged by the importers with an Indian underwriter. The consignment, when opened at final destination was found with chalk powder and was not having uniform quantity inside the HDPE drums. However, externally the pilfer proof seals were intact. The loss was reported by the importers to their overseas suppliers and to their local underwriter as well.

A surveyor was appointed by overseas underwriter to confirm if the loss had taken place during air travel. The surveyor had opined that the consignment was cleared without any abnormal finding from the Mumbai airport and since it was carried through a locality with antisocial elements known for indulging in notorious activities, the loss had taken place after being discharged from the airport. Hence the liability should fall on the local underwriters.

The local underwriters in turn appointed a famous surveyor (famous for not wanting to be famous) to conduct an in-depth survey of the consignment. The learned surveyor who had remarkable intensity in his eyes, after comparing the present consignment with the previous sound consignments masterfully confirmed that the HDPE drums in question were apparently similar but not the same. And neither the look-alike drums nor the chalk powder were of Indian make. Thus it was proved with impeccable correctness that the original drums along with the original contents were replaced from the port of dispatch. Thus overseas underwriters should be liable for the loss.

If insurers appoint the right kind of surveyor, they shall get the right kind of report. Only when insurers are upright, they appoint right kind of surveyors.

Chasis prints: hand-made and machine-made

The insured approached for renewal of his Toyota Qualis. As per existing procedure, the branch officials asked for a copy of registration certificate, renewal notice and physical inspection of the vehicle. The insured produced a photocopy of cover note issued by Delhi office of another company showing expiry date of policy falling after ten days. And the vehicle too was produced for inspection. Branch officials physically inspected the said vehicle and obtained chassis number print on the proposal form and since the number got tallied with the RC book, insurance coverage was granted.

Three months later a claim on the same vehicle was reported at the branch office. The insured informed in writing that since the loss was extensive, they had arranged spot survey through a local surveyor. Final surveyor was deputed by regional office who conducted the survey and submitted his report.

One day the insured's representative came to the regional office along with two gunmen with the intention to pressurize for immediate settlement of the claim. It was a nerve-wracking experience for the regional manager. But such unruly behaviour created doubt. On insightful scrutiny it was noticed that the chassis number obtained on the proposal form although was tallying, the shape and size of the digits and alphabets were different from the chassis print taken by the final surveyor. One was haphazard and hand-made and the other one was meticulous and machine-made. The anomaly was too serious to be overlooked.

The original cover note copy of the previous underwriter was called for. It was confirmed that the cover note validity period had been tampered with and actually the previous policy had expired six months before the date of renewal. Further a net of salvage claim of Rs 5 lakh had been settled by them on the same vehicle. Finally it was brought to light that the insured had managed to punchmark his damaged vehicle's chassis number on another similar vehicle and had produced the same for physical verification with damaged vehicle's number plates removed and fixed on it.

Finally the insured was informed about the truth and was advised to withdraw the claim. The Insured roared like a cornered tiger for a while and was never seen again.

Adverse impact of pressure

It was 10 pm in Shirpur city. All shops had been closed for the day. Just opposite to a certain police station a huge tyre shop was insured for Rs 2 crore. A big truck appeared from nowhere and parked itself almost covering the shop. A number of people got down from the vehicle and started making the noise of repairing the truck. When police officials came, they only saw the activities of repairing. But in the midst of repairing noise, they kept cutting the locks, opened the shutter and started some kind of loading as if it was part of their normal business activity.

The morning next, the claim of burglary was reported by the owner of the same shop to the insurance office and thus a surveyor was rushed to the spot. Police report and other relevant papers were submitted. An assessment of Rs 1 crore came without much delay with all the invoices attached. When the regional manager who was a cut above others in intelligence was unusually pressurized, he telephoned the surveyor to go and verify the invoices with the suppliers and report its genuineness. After exactly one hour the surveyor confirmed over the telephone that the invoices were verified and were found in order. The speed at which he did the job was ominous. This sparked curiosity in the mind of regional manager because the distance between the city of the suppliers and the city of the surveyor was about 150 km, and how was it possible for him to travel such long distance and verify the invoices in just one hour's time ?

He telephoned another surveyor in the supplier's city to collect copies of relevant invoices from the regional office and get them verified. On verification it was found that the delivery of the tyres relating to those invoices was not taken by the insured because the necessary payments had not been made. Only the invoices had been raised and sent because the insured wanted to meet certain target to get some incentive but later on he could neither make payment nor take delivery. Had the insured not pressurized too much, the claim in normal course might have got settled like many other such claims.

Some rusty reasons to suspect

A picture speaks a thousand words. And a photograph still more because it directly comes from the object. But words do not because a word is human creation. Reports are full of words, full of so many interpretations and so many explanations. But a picture represents truth. This is equally true when a claim manager sees rust in the cuts and dents in the photos of a damaged vehicle. Here is a stunning example of how through astute observation of the photographs and deductive reasoning, the prudent manager doubted that the accident was not fresh because the wounds on the steel body had rusted enough. He felt drawn towards the rust and investigated to find that the honourable man had purchased two similar vehicles together: one in his name and the other in the name of his beloved wife. These vehicles were insured with two different companies. His vehicle met with an accident and after obtaining the claim on net of salvage basis, he had fixed the number plates of his wife's vehicle to the damaged one and was trying to take the second claim. Because of the time gap of two months between two claims the fresh wounds on the steel body had rusted. Photographs of the previous accident were obtained from the other insurance company. They were found to be the same except the number plates and rust marks.

When confronted with the truth, the insured's husband gave a withered look equal to the withered condition of his manipulated claim and disappeared. Photographs are more authentic than the survey report and thus must be seen with forensic eyes. We too should have a space in the proposal form asking for the colour of the car which should in turn be recorded in the policy to prevent such double claims for a single accident. Sometimes accident takes place during break-in-insurance period, the insured manages to obtain a cover and waits for a month or so to lodge his claim especially in case of private cars where police reports are not necessary. In such cases rust appears on damage portion of the body which can lead to deciphering the truth behind the claim.

Preventing erosion of confidence

A surveyor is the most vital person in insurance administration but once he makes the assessment, he feels that his job is over. He has in fact many functions. He has to see the underwriting aspects whether the claim falls under the scope of the policy or not. He has claim minimization functions like advising the insured to maximize salvaging of damaged items. He has the functions of a mediator making both the Insured and the underwriter agree to the assessment. And advisory functions like what precautionary measures the Insured has to take to prevent such losses in future and what covers he should opt for to get full indemnity at the time of loss.

A surveyor's casual approach can cause erosion of confidence and trust. For example a hydro power plant was damaged in a flash flood. The insured lodged a claim for Rs 100 crore. The project was co-insured with another underwriter on 55:45 basis. The lead insurer appointed a reputed surveyor since the claim was huge. The co-insurer thought it proper to appoint their surveyor too. Both the surveyors took two years collecting various documents and demanded double the fees for the complicated nature of the claim. During co-insurance premium settlement it came to light that **Contractors' All Risk** policy had expired three months before the date of accident and the Insured had not taken further extension. In short two long years of labour was lost in vain. Every time a surveyor gets a job, he should read and re- read the policy to find out the scope of cover in relation to the claim.

In another case the insurance was taken only for the new Chasis. After body of the vehicle was built, the insured had forgotten to take insurance for the body. Unfortunately the vehicle met with a severe accident and without seeing the scope of the cover the surveyor blindly recommended to compensate the loss to the body also and submitted his report. The file majestically sailed through branch and division. Only at regional office the anomaly was noticed and the assessment was put to correction. Such examples throw into sharp focus that much more is expected from a surveyor than a casual assessment of the loss. A survey report is the fulcrum on which the good and bad images of the insurance industry are balanced. Thus a surveyor needs to execute his task with sincerity and grace.

Insurance Then and Now

Year: 1700 BC. Place: A village in Egypt where thirty farmers lived. Every summer each farmer used to build a haystack so that he could feed his cows during winter. Towards the end of each summer there were thunderstorms and sometimes lightning used to set the haystacks on fire. When this happened, the unlucky farmer used to buy hay from his neighbour to save his cows from starvation.

It dawned upon one wise farmer that though he made little money selling hay to other farmers who lost their haystacks, he would be ruined if he lost his own. So he said to his neighbour, 'We should agree that if either of us loses his haystack, we shall share one that is safe'. This way third farmer also joined the group and then the rest of the villagers. When lightning used to strike, the insured and the insurer were from among the same persons who decided the loss and compensated. Everything was very simple.

Times have changed. Risks have become complicated, man's mind more complicated and the ways of the world most complicated. With unprecedented underwriting losses and fire and engineering premium rates slashed by 80%, insurance industry has certainly been pushed to the wall. Let the underwriters move into a new sensitivity, into new intelligence to sharpen their skills and respond quickly in arriving at the assessment. Depending entirely on surveyors is a nineteenth century method which cannot meet 21st century needs. And the claim managers cannot afford to distance themselves from visiting the site of claims. And insurers have to change, they have the potentiality to deliver change. Yes, they need this extra cover for the covers they grant. Otherwise they shall be perpetually in red. And red is bad for business.

CHAPTER 12

Impact of Road Rules in School Syllabus

"Accidents do not happen accidentally.
We cause it to happen."

- Confucius

It was in the year 2001. Despite age related illness, a 50 seater fifteen year old bus with all retreaded tyres, driven by the helper sans skill and sans license coming from countryside to the city picked up **103** passengers on the way, and due to overage, overloading and over-speeding spiralled out of control, fell from the bridge from a height of fifty feet and crashed on the dry summer bed of the river killing everyone. Almost all norms that would normally make the vehicle safe on the road were flouted. Such accidents trigger deep disquiet for a while and are forgotten. Confucius is right when he says, such accidents are not accidental but entirely a man-made affair. Twin towers tragedy which killed 3,400 people on 9/11 made the whole world sit up and take note with bated breaths. But the world will be shocked out of its wits to know that more than 3,400 people die and more than thrice that number get maimed in road accidents across the globe every day. But to our utter dismay, neither for the individuals nor for the nations have this startling statistics aroused any concern to prevent such recurring disaster. Gujarat cyclone took **26,000** lives and Orissa cyclone claimed **20,000**. In our own country more than one lakh people die every year and three lakh get seriously injured on killer roads. Despite such enormous casualties, we are totally insensitive to this more shocking national disaster. It is sad to note that an emergency situation like this has been accepted as natural happening especially when with pouring in of innumerable new vehicles, the road accident toll soars up like barometer in hot summer desert.

Child is father of the man

It is famously said that child is father of the man. When children talk to their parents to drive slow, put on helmets, fasten seat belts and not to use mobile phone while driving, they would listen and obey. Hence, if the child learns, parents will learn too. Moreover, every child holds in him or her the adult of tomorrow and the parent of day after tomorrow. By giving road safety education to school children we can lay a strong foundation on which the superstructure of traffic discipline can be built which in turn will reduce accidents. It too will mould them in moral education. When they become RTAs, they would think thrice before issuing driving licenses without testing driving skills. When they become fleet owners, they will think thrice before sending their trucks overloaded. At the age of 14 a child's mind-set and personality take complete shape. This period is vital in man's life. Whatever he learns now remains riveted in his mind forever. As the Arbian proverb says "Knowledge acquired as a child is more lasting than engraving on stone".

In our country more and more adolescents die in two wheeler accidents. One because of the speed they drive at, two, because that age their mind is not on a tight leash. Dharampal Singh, 17, a class XII student in Delhi was dropping his sister Ipsita Kaur 13 who studied in class VII. Both of them fell from the bike while trying to avoid a vendor, came under the rear wheel of a speeding bus and died on the spot. This horrific death, besides snuffing out young lives, got seared in the emotional memory of their loving parents. Such incidents are many and rather heart-breakingly pathetic. It is for the students to take note of it in the unforgettable corner of their memories. Loving parents giving bikes to the children must compulsorily attach side cars to cool the youthful energy of their children and tone down their youthful exuberance.

More important than many unwanted subjects

Traffic discipline as a tool is used by every individual everyday once she or he is out of home as a driver, as a passenger or as a pedestrian. Hence, to remain ignorant of road rules is too serious to be excused. How much do the information of history, Machiavellian theories of politics and abstract theories of mathematics and economics help man in living his daily life? Too much unnecessary information is being fed to children now-a-days. On the other hand, knowledge on traffic discipline will be useful in every moment of man's life.

The role and benefit of insurance industry

To reduce accidents means to bring down claims. The outgo of the insurance companies is more than Rs.20,000 crore towards motor claims every year. They should hold frequent educative programs and arrange to produce high quality documentary films on road safety for the school children. If road accidents are reduced, they would certainly benefit by way of low claim payouts.

If the motor pool spends Rs 100 crore in this regard, the insurance industry will benefit in thousands of crore both now and in future. Once accidents are reduced, claims too will be reduced. Once claims are reduced, the rate of premium will be reduced. Thus importance of educating children on road safety should not be ignored. Let us devote some of our weekends in holding road safety programs in schools. Let the industry divert its huge advertisement budgets to educate children on safety lessons. The returns shall be manifold by way of prevention of accidents and saving of god-gifted lives. This way we shall be more prayerful without visiting places of worship. An then buying motor insurance will be wallet-friendly.

Need for institutes of driver education

Any other education may go waste but lessons on safe driving will not. In the year 2009-10, total 15,15,880 passengers vehicles, 3,84,122 commercial vehicles, 3,49,719 three wheelers and 74,37,670 two wheelers were sold in our country which make a total of about one crore vehicles. Whether we have adequate number of driving schools to train an equal number of drivers every year is a topic of serious concern. Moreover the fact that one can get a driving license without any skill test in our country contributes greatly to accidents. People responsible for this get away with impunity after making mincemeat of existing laws.

Insurance industry (which has been blinded to this horrendous act in pursuit of growth) a should give a thought to this issue and liberally invest in establishing large number of institutes of driver education in imparting skills and self-discipline which it will financially benefit from in the long run. And our roads shall be less and less prone to accidents, thus paving the way for a society which will be accident-free and hence blissful.

Ensuring driver's welfare

Most of the accidents are caused by the negligence of the drivers. Be it their lack of skill, be it their falling asleep while at the wheel, be it their thinking of personal problems while driving or be it their rash and negligent driving, all contribute to the cause of accident. Looking after the driver's welfare is the prime duty of the vehicle owner. One may be having a Mercedes but if the driver is underpaid, the atmosphere inside the car will be inhospitable and uncomfortable and there will be an open invitation to accident.

Say no to Late-Night-Journey

Real life stories of road accidents and their consequences should be narrated in the school. For example, many families who had started to distant places at midnight, had met with horrific accidents at wee hours of the day and instantly died. Kulkarni family of Belgaum had started their journey by car at 11pm in the night for Tirupati. At 5 am in the morning their car met with an accident and most of them died on the spot. Das family after marriage ceremony in Behrampur started their return journey at 11.55 pm at night on Wednesday (since next day i.e. Thursday was considered inauspicious for return journey) to Rourkela. At 5.30 in the morning near Dhenkanal their car dashed against a trailer appearing suddenly from across the roadside *dhaba*. The driver of the car in his effort to keep his drooping eyelids wide open was driving at reckless speed of 120 km per hour. The accident was so severe that the heads of all the passengers were separated from their body and were thrown 40 ft away. Driving over the speed does not really save time but accelerates tension in geometrical progression and at times ends up with fatal consequences.

A driver is a human being. He will feel sleepy at late night as much as the passengers would. Why not rest whole night and begin the journey after in the morning. The principle should be the same for the return journey. Every year we hear buses carrying marriage parties meeting with serious accidents. The driver who was sleepless night before has to drive long distance the morning after with eyelids drooping down heavy with sleep. That is precisely why the unfortunate incidents occur. Our society takes no care of the driver. It is highly deplorable.

In Punjab it is said, drink only at a place where you have decided to sleep. If you feel sleepy while driving, park your vehicle on the safe side of the road and sleep for a while, then re-start. Do not increase your speed to overtake. If some fellow cars are overtaken by your normal speed, that is just fine. Many such lessons can be given to school children at various levels especially at X, XI and XII - which will leave indelible impressions on their young minds.

Say no to burning vehicles

Say no to burning vehicles to express your anger. Who pays for such claims? Insurance companies do not pay from their pockets. They pay it from the premium collected. Who pays the premium. The public. More the claims, higher is the rate of premium. Finally it costs the public more money. It is almost always the human error that causes accident. The vehicle itself does not. Because it cannot protest, because it cannot run away on its own, we set it on fire. They are soft targets. We burn not one but many at a time. No doubt insurance companies pay for the loss but ultimately they recover it by increasing the rate of premium. Find out peaceful alternatives to express your protest.

Let us give it a good start

Be it out of ignorance in case of village folks, be it out of impulse in case of adolescents, be it out of fatigue in case of long distance drivers, be it the drunken driver faltering on midnight streets, be it the helper driving out of temptation, be it the owners of transport companies engaging semi-skilled drivers throwing safety to the wind, be it owners of the ill- maintained vehicles, proper education on traffic rules is the right preventive solution to these gigantic problems. Only through intense education to all concerned on traffic safety, the pernicious situation can be pre-empted. And there cannot be a better place to introduce curriculum on road safety than in schools. A detailed syllabus should be designed with the help of industry and automobile experts along with video clippings of real life cases to get this most valuable message tattooed in their thought- process. Road safety education is fundamental to sustain lives in this world. Let us make it universal and compulsory, for God's sake please !

CHAPTER 13

Stock Claims: Challenges

Down the years stock claims have baffled the insurance executives like branch managers, divisional managers and regional managers. At times claims arising out of arson have unknowingly been paid and forgotten; and claims inflated by 1000% have been settled without ripples. One does not have to become a chartered accountant to understand the stock claims because Taj Mahal, one of the seven wonders of the world, was not built by any civil engineer. Visit to the site, presence of mind, love for your job and basic intelligence will enable the claim manager to see through a stock claim. What has been happening in the industry is that public sector insurance executives appoint the surveyor for claim assessment and then just forget. When the report comes after one year or so with an invisible accusing fingure at them for delay, they hasten to process the claim for settlement with very little scope for pointing out the bogus from the real at that stage. Here is a real case study alongwith step-by-step analysis as to how to handle stock claims which will be of some use to the insurance officials.

Types of fraud

Frauds in stock claims can be classified under three heads. Opportunis- tic frauds are those where an honest insured gets tempted to inflate an otherwise genuine claim.

Conspiratorial frauds are all about an insured conspiring to commit a fraud by taking exaggerated sum insured for a little or negligible stock. Compensatory frauds are noticed when because of market slumps the insured commits arson on a huge inventory. Although the first two can be tackled through investigation, the third, of course, is very difficult to prove. Handling stock claim is tough because fire to the building and machinery will not destroy everything. Salvage in such cases will be available and will determine the existence of the property before fire. As the fire on stock can reduce everything to ashes, to estimate the volume of stock existed before occurrence of fire is a tough call to make. Yet, like they say, where there is a will, there is a way.

A real-life case study to drive home the point

A plastic granules manufacturing company suddenly took insurance in the month of May1999 as follows:

Stock   :   Rs 80 lakh

Building   :   Rs 10 lakh

Machinery :   Rs 26 lakh

Although the plant was installed between November 1998 to March

1999, there was no erection all risks insurance. In morning of 29 December 1999 there was a blazing fire in the factory.

Step one: Visiting the Site

Intelligence works neither in the past nor in future. It always works in the present. Therefore, immediate visit to the site of fire (which public sector companies unfortunately do not do) by the team of claim officials is like a stitch in time that saves nine. Well, in the subject case the team visited. On enquiry, it was found that the insured was out of town when the fire took place. It may not always be a coincidence. But it is a common psychology that an arsonist does not prefer to stay at the site of arson. Hence the initial seeds of suspicion got germinated in the minds of the visiting team.

That apart, the control panel from where the fire was

alleged to have originated did not have any medium for the fire to spread to the machiner y and stock. There was 20 feet vacant space among these sections. The installation of machinery and storage of stock had gap enough from the electrical wiring on the wall not to come in contact with any electrical fire.

The giant step

The insured claimed the amount in full. To ascertain the volume of the insured's business transaction, the verification of his bank statement (known in accounting parlance as cash flow statement or known in a rustic language as pass book) was under any circumstances an indispensable necessity. Because unlike a pass book, most other documents could be manipulated (mercifully, bankers enjoy that kind of credibility in this country). This undoubtedly could give a clear picture of how much payment he made for the purchase of raw material and how much money he received from the sale of finished products on monthly basis. In the case under study, although the sum insured opted was Rs 80 lakh, his monthly transactions on both ways were only to the extent of about Rs 2 lakh. Hence the misgivings intensified. Even when he had proposed his stock worth Rs 80 lakh for insurance, his monthly transaction was only Rs 3 lakh.

The evidence

Next step was to check the electricity bill. Since it was a power-oriented unit, consumption of electricity would give a fair amount of idea of most of the activity. In the case under study the electricity consumption barring one month was nil. Hence the suspicions grew intense. The most significant and irrefutable piece of evidence was the meter reading of the unit during the preceding seven months prior to fire. The bills submitted by the insured had a remark by the electricity department as H/C which means "house closed". In the absence of electricity consumption no production was possible. Further with the house closed there must not have been any production activity. These startling details were too glaring to be wished away and hence strengthened the apprehension.

Final moment of truth

The truth in its pristine form came from the verification of purchase invoices. The surveyor, a mechanical engineer, without going into the heart of the matter, had aggregated the amount of all purchase bills and had assessed the amount at Rs 80 lakh as loss. The reason for the sudden outbreak of generosity by the surveyor was best known to himself. Invoices worth Rs 50 lakh pertaining to purchase of raw material in the month just before the fire was sent for investigation. The investigator could produce documentary evidence from the sales tax commissioners from the related cities to the effect that neither the parties existed nor the sales tax numbers in the invoices did confirm to the pattern as allotted by the sales tax department. The investigator proved that the invoices were from the non-existent sellers. The claim was crafted and fake and thus was repudiated as per condition no. 8 of the fire policy:

'If the claim be in any respect fraudulent or if any false declaration be made or used in support thereof or the damage be occasioned by any willful act….all benefits under the policy shall be forfeited.'

Such claims clog up the system and choke off the portfolio. Recently in UK the insurance industry has set up Insurance Fraud Bureau (IFB) to counter organized fraud by co-coordinating investigations and building relationship with law enforcement agencies. The IFB estimates to have saved GBP 8 million for the industry in first year of its operation in 2006 leading to 74 arrests so far. It has also set up facilities for the members of the public to report suspicious activities. Its battle against fraudsters has given a major boost to the Association of British Insurers (ABI).

Sadly, there has not been any conscious effort by the industry in this respect in our country. It is suggested that IRDA should come out with such arrangement to plug leakages amounting to thousands of crores. Prevention of fraud must be closer to the heart of the industry. Reducing the cost of claims without ill-treating the customers should be the top priority in insurers' agenda. Most of the insurance companies are incurring heavy underwriting losses. With fire premium getting reduced to an all-time low, prevention of fraud in stock claims must move from a casual back-office administrative chore to a key business activity. Time we sharpen our tools !

CHAPTER 14

Misuse of Jewellery Insurance

Beauty of Jewellry has the ugly side of giving come-hither look to thieves. At the same time it is nothing unless put on and exhibited. But while exuding its glamour and brightness, it has always to be protected with utmost alertness. Jewelry like beauty, is always a risky item. It is even more risky when it moves from one place to another. Like Helen of Troy, its very beauty is liable to launch a thousand misdeeds. Like a man should be brave enough to possess Helen, the insured should be careful enough while taking his jewelry from one place to another because once snatched away the jewelry is gone forever. Once he is absent minded, it disappears within seconds. Its theft may not create a horrible scene like a house on fire or motor vehicle disintegrated in an accident but being very costly, a not-so-violent event of theft in transit becomes a huge burden on the underwriters. Moreover, it occurs at strange places among the strangers leaving little scope to verify the occurrence of loss because there would be no evidence left.

All over the country jewelry stores are insured for hundreds of millions of rupees. Genuine claims have been paid without any hassle for the similar amount by the underwriters. In fact, jewellers cannot open their shop even for a day without insurance coverage because premium is so little and transfer of risk to the underwriters is so huge. But here are some of real life happenings that appear to be more artfully orchestrated than haplessly accidental.

Key factor

Once an insured in a metro city had taken an all risk insurance policy for his high value jewelry. Some of the jewelry was kept in the locker with a nationalized bank. One day for attending a family function, the insured took out some high value solitaire diamond jewelry worth Rs 50 lakh from the locker. On his way back home he parked his high value limousine near a market place, carefully locked it and went to a medicine store to buy some medicine. After returning he opened the car and found that the jewelry placed inside the car was missing. Immediately he started searching everywhere inside the car but could not find it. Subsequently he lodged an FIR with the nearest police station and thereafter preferred a claim with his insurer. The under writing office after completion of all formalities recommended the claim for settlement to the competent authority.

Since the jewelry was stolen from a high value and high tech. car and no forcible entry was noticed, the competent authority referred the matter to the manufacturer of the car who in response opined that it was impossible to open the car using any key other than the one supplied by them because it had an inbuilt sensor. Thus, it was inferred that there was no forcible entry into the car and it was reasonably concluded that the claim did not fall within the scope of the policy. Accordingly, claim was repudiated by the insurance company.

Technical reasons apart, the insured would certainly not have left such high value items in unsafe situation had it not been insured. A prudent insured would have carried the jewelry with him to the medicine store because it was very small in size and hence portable enough to be carried along. It is not an afterthought because such minimum caution was expected to be taken by a prudent insured.

Unlocked doors

The proprietor of a jewellry firm covered under jewellers' block policy was carrying five sets of diamond necklaces from his shop located at Dadar in Mumbai to his residence at Andheri in his own car to show his neighbour who was supposed to buy one of the necklaces. He was alone and himself driving the car. He reached Santa Cruz around 8.30 pm and was idling his engine at a red signal. At that very moment one un-known person knocked at the car window and drew his attention. He was indicating something by hand to the rear side as if tyres were deflated. The insured opened the door and came outside, examined the rear tyres and found them intact. When he returned and entered the car, he noticed that bag in which diamond necklace sets were kept on front seat was missing. In the meantime, traffic signal became green. The person who indicated and knocked had melted in the crowd obliterating any possibility of tracking him. He drove forward and parked the car on the left side of the road and frisked the inside of the whole car. The bag containing five diamond necklace sets could not be traced. He immediately rushed to the nearby police station and lodged a written complaint.

Some insurance pundits argue that to come out of the car was a natural response on the part of the insured while others are of the opinion that the insured could have locked all the doors with automatic locking system which the car had by pressing the button in the key before coming to check the rear wheels. They also argue that he could have kept the bag in the boot of the car duly locked or he could have taken that little bag along with him while coming out to check the alleged deflected wheels. The surveyor had concluded that at the time of theft, stock was lying in the car with doors unlocked and insured was not present in car with the stock. Theft took place from un-attended bag kept in the car because the insured was outside the car for checking tyres. At the material time of theft there was no one to resist the theft.

He cited policy exclusion no.5 of the jewellers block policy which stipulates, "Theft of stock from un-attended vehicle is not covered under the policy" and at the material time of theft that the stock was left un-attended in the vehicle was also confessed by the insured in writing in police complaint. Hence the claim was outside the scope of insurance coverage.

Lost for lust

A wholesaler of gold jewellery had insured his shop under jewellers' block policy. He had sent three of his salesmen with gold jewellery worth Rs 80 lakh to Bangalore for sale. They travelled by bus and reached Bangalore the day next. After reaching they stayed in a hotel and then they visited a few jewelers to negotiate the sale. But they were not successful in selling even a single piece of jewellery. The insured directed them to return. They arranged tickets and traveled back the same night but in the next morning, when the bus stopped at motel Oasis in Pune-Mumbai express highway, all three salesmen alighted from the bus and were standing nearby. In the meantime, one of the staff members saw that one person was taking away a box in a plastic carry-bag similar to their jewellery box. After recognizing their own box, he shouted to the other two colleagues that the person was taking away their own jewellery box. They all ran after that person who in turn ran faster towards the parking area. One staff caught the collar of the culprit but the later gave a push to him and ran towards the Alto car parked nearby with engine on. Inside the car one person was already sitting. He entered the car with box and they together drove away with jewellery on express highway. Rs 80 lakhs of jewellery disappeared in seconds.

After that they returned to the bus and saw that the thief had broken the VIP suitcase which was locked and fixed to the the seat with a chain. They reported the incident to police station. The police arrived at the place of incident, recorded their statement and registered the FIR.

As per the surveyor's opinion, at the time of theft, stock

was lying in the bus but no employee of insured was present in the bus to take care of the jewellery. Theft took place from un-attended bag kept in the bus. Three employees of insured were carrying stock but no one was there at the time of theft to resist the theft. This claim was rejected as per the exclusion of the policy. It was okay to travel in a public transport but less okay to leave the jewellery unattended. This indeed was unfortunate. Hence the claim was not payable.

The underwriters should put suitable warranty that such incidents should happen because of the gross negligence of the insured or his representative. Hence an explicit and appropriate warranty should be incorporated in the policy not with the intention of not paying the claim but to make the insured aware of his duties and responsibilities during the operation of the insurance policy.

Who on earth would believe that it was a rare co-incidence for thieves to know that a bus would arrive, at this place, at this time and on this seat a jewellery box will be inside the VIP suitcase. Such incidences of careless handling would discourage the underwriters to extend the cover or if at all the cover is to be given it should be with due diligence warranty.

Height of carelessness

In the morning of 8 October 2001, while holidaying

at a nearby hill station, the insured got a telephone call that his jewellery shop had been burgled around 2 am in the morning. Immediately he rushed back and found that two locks of the north side shutter of his shop had been broken open. On scrutiny he found that the jewellery worth Rs 2 crore that were kept in the wooden drawers of the sales counter and Rs 10 lakh cash that was kept in the wooden drawer of cash counter had been stolen. He thereafter went to the police station and lodged an FIR stating the fact about the theft and intimated to the underwriters along with an original copy of the FIR. The underwriters visited the site of burglary along with an investigator and a surveyor. On scrutiny during inspection it was noticed that the CCTV cameras were switched off at the time of burglary, the burglar alarm had not been in place, the wooden drawers in both the sales counter and in the cash counter had been broken and the contents alleged to have been taken away as mentioned in the FIR. But the safe in which the valuables were supposed to have been kept at the time of theft, was intact and was untouched by the unwanted visitors.

The underwriters had a meeting with both the surveyor and the investigator and obtained necessary reports immediately. On the receipt of the same and on the basis of the FIR filed by the insured, they intimated in writing to the insured that the claim was not payable because policy clearly said "warranted that all property including cash and currency notes whilst at the premises specified in the schedule shall be secured in locked safe of standard make at all times after business hours." The insured got the shock of his life on receipt of the no-claim-letter and tried unsuccessfully to change the FIR stating that the jewellery and cash were in the safe at the time of theft. No one knew what really had happened but everybody knew what was obvious.

Fraud is a serious and expensive problem faced by both insurance companies and insurance buying public. Insurance is based on the principle that each insured makes a fair contribution to the pool from which the many pay losses for a few. But such claims which are fortunes for the few, amount to killing the golden goose. Therefore such practices demand extra intelligence to do moral hazard underwriting and bring fraudulent claims to light.

CHAPTER 15

Teachers open the door; you enter by yourself.
Chinese Proverb

Claims that every Underwriter must Know

Poetically but most appropriately Walter M Mellert the famous Swiss underwriter has put it that underwriting tools - no matter how cleverly devised - are only tools. They are like brush without a painter, chisel without a carpenter, rifle without a responsible marksman and are all just inanimate objects. In the hands of the inexperienced, such tools may even become dangerous to your health or property or someone else's. No underwriting tool will ever replace the overall assessment of all risk factors done by an underwriter using all available intellectual and emotional faculties to arrive at the right decision.

Casual underwriting: a recipe for disaster

In a market where there is no punishment for lodging bogus claims, there can develop a natural instinct for a failed businessman to create claims through arson (as happened during recession) or to exaggerate a genuine claim or to obtain policy on happened losses without any fear of punitive consequences.

Decades back an immaculately dressed businessman entered an insurance office in New Delhi at 4.30 pm and asked for an in-land-transit cover. The consignment consisted of four small aircrafts carried in a huge trailer truck valued at Rs 2 crore which was to cover a distance of 518.8 kms from New Delhi, the place of dispatch to Kanpur, the delivery destination. He paid Rs 30,000. premium in cash and managed to have a cover note issued. The unsuspecting underwriter could neither read the happening behind those worried eyes of the insured nor could he decipher the restlessness of his body language but did not forget to put 5 pm as the time of issuance of the cover note.

The next day, the underwriters who had failed to see through the intention of the Insured, were shocked to receive a claim intimation stating that the two of the aircrafts were totally burnt, the other two were partially damaged due to short circuit since the aircrafts came in contact with the low lying overhead electric wires at

9 pm last night. And this accident had taken place 250 km away from the place of dispatch.

A surveyor was appointed to assess the loss. What was more discomfiting for the claim officials was that insurance was taken at 5 pm and accident took place at 9 pm. How could a slow moving trailer loaded with such delicate cargo as four aircrafts would cover a distance of 250 km in just four hours that too during night time? Hence it kicked up a storm and triggered a wave of dissent. But in an overt attempt to prove his point, the insured submitted all relevant documents including police and fire brigade reports justifying that the accident had taken place at 9 pm on the very date after taking insurance.

Troubled by doubts the claim officials were instinctively agitated and appointed an investigator. Video recordings of eye witnesses were taken confirming that the fire accident had taken place at 2 pm before taking insurance and not at 9 pm. But this was not enough ammunition to counter the proof submitted by the insured in favor of his claim because the insured had quite effectively managed to get the reports issued by government agencies in his favor. It was an onerous job to prove the claimant wrong. But the investigator stumbled upon one evidence which had not been secreted out and that worked as coup de grace. It was the fire brigade entry and exit register that recorded that the fire tenders left the fire station at 2.20

pm to the place of accident to douse fire. Thus the cat finally came out of the bag and the claim was repudiated decisively. It is not easy to reject a claim because it invites scorn and disdain of the insured. But it was too difficult to take a decision to the contrary.

But underwriting such a risk is a recipe for disaster. Obtaining insurance after the accident is not specific to transit insurance alone. It also happens in fire, burglary and other kinds of insurances. But the underwriter has to be intuitive and shall have the knowledge of psychology to see the invisible and avoid such proposals because our business is to cover future risks not to insure occurred losses. Insurance is a noble service ensuring stability. But such claims try to destabilise the very foundation of insurance.

Learning underwriting from claims

Take for instance a certain company in a metro city had been importing tin plate coils from Korea which used to have been insured for Rs 9,000 per metric ton against institute cargo clauses (all risks). On every consignment there was claim due to rust and 30 to 40 % allowance was given to the insured because the same could not be used as containers for food items, the purpose for which it was imported. One day it came to the knowledge of the underwriters that the rust-damaged tin plate coils were much in demand and were sold @Rs 12,000 per metric ton in the market and were safely used as containers for paints. Thus every time the insured was making big profit from insurance claims. For the subsequent claims the intelligent claim manager stewed over the issue for some time and decided to keep the salvage and settle the claim on total loss basis thereby ensuring for his company a profit of about Rs 3,000 in every ton of rusted tin plate coil claim. But the insured vehemently disagreed to this arrangement. Since the insured was an old customer, it was mutually agreed to insure future consignments excluding rust damage for which

30% discount on premium rates was allowed. It was a win–win situation for both the parties. Insurance company getting rid of recurrent claims and the insured paying less premium.

Lesson for the future

A government institution approached the underwriters to insure their camera worth Rs 2 crore on all risks basis. The insurers quoted 2% rate. The insured's representatives insisted bare minimum cover for formality sake just because their auditors were insisting for insurance. The camera was fixed on a van and it used to take snaps of rivers, landscapes, buildings and meadows. Since clients were insisting on minimum coverage, the insurance company offered the cover @

0.25% but with the conditions that damage to the camera would be paid only when the van would be damaged in accident. Tempted by the low rate of premium, the clients' representatives went overboard in their enthusiasm of saving Rs 3.5 lakh premium and agreed in writing for this condition.

Policy ran very well for six months. The insured used the camera by fixing it on a van and took many snaps. One fine morning, they decided to fix this camera on a piece of wooden plank and then attached it to helicopter with a long rope. The helicopter was flown over jungles of the state and this camera captured beautiful snaps of pathless spots. One afternoon the helicopter lost the height. The wooden plank on which camera was fixed got struck up among the trees and started pulling helicopter down. The pilot immediately removed the hook to which string was attached to save the helicopter. The camera fell from a big height and got smashed into pieces. Insured lodged the claim for Rs 2 crore. The insurance company denied its liability politely saying that helicopter was not a van.

With tacit show of nervousness clients' representatives argued a lot but the company officials showed DGCA report saying that there was neither any damage to any passenger nor to the helicopter. They reminded the clients of the written condition that the damage to camera would be payable provided the van was also damaged. Even if the contention that helicopter was a vehicle, it was not affected either. Hence the claim was not tenable. The clients were politely reminded of their inappropriate assessment of the risk. This case can stir undercurrent among the insurance customers in the world who are unknowingly in the habit of being exposed to far greater risks in the name of saving little bit of premium that is miniscule fraction of the huge potential loss.

CHAPTER 16

Rare Claims from Archives

Insurance fraud seriously affects the entire class of honest policy holders in terms of increase in premium rates. It is easy for the insured to commit fraud but it is in no way easy for the underwriters to detect that fraud. Again, if the underwriter alleges that the insured has lodged a bogus claim, the burden of proving the same rests with the underwriter. It is nearly impossible to prove that the claim is fraudulent beyond all reasonable doubts because in such cases the degree of proof has been quantified in mathematical terms as 90 % in contrast to the proof in civil cases which is 51 %.

But nothing is impossible if one has the right kind of determination and passion for the job. Here are some real life cases where the dedicated insurance officials have been intuitive enough to take the skeleton out of the cupboard; and some have helped the insured to take his rightful claims that apparently looked falling beyond the scope of coverage.

Inside the banker's blanket

Non-life claims are not simple and straight. For example, Bank B had issued a draft for Rs 9,000 to C. Mr. C in turn got nine lakh in words and 90 in figures smoothly eased into the little spaces left in the pre-fix sides to make the draft amount read as Rs 9,09,000 (nine lakh nine thousand only) and encashed it immediately. When the matter came to light after a month, the insured bank lodged a claim for the difference amount of Rs 9 lakh under the bankers' blanket policy with the underwriters.

A surveyor was appointed. He thoroughly investigated the matter and assessed the loss for Rs 9 lakh and recommended for payment establishing the liability of the insurance company. On scrutiny, the following anomalies were noticed by the insurane officials in the said draft. That proper taping of the amount in figures and words was not done so that same could not have been altered later on. The bank should have ensured that proper punching of the draft was done. Further on the face of the draft a stamping of not more than

Rs...... should have been incorporated to nullify any fraudulent changes.

But all these factors were not sufficient enough to absolve the insurance company of its liability. Pressure mounted on the insurance officials for settlement of the claim and the divisional office recommended the claim to higher office for necessary sanction.

In regional office one officer who had insightful intelligence could find something which made everyone sit up and take notice. He found from the photocopy of the concerned bank draft which was submitted by the surveyor for ready reference that the draft was prepared as account payee which means C would have to compulsorily deposit the draft in his bank account to encash the same. Immediately the bank through which C had encashed his draft was informed by the insured bank, an FIR was filed and C was traced and arrested. Recovery procedure started. The underwriters were absolved of their liability by writing a polite letter of no claim.

Fraudsters always leave behind some clues for the intelligent eyes to detect the fraud. There are no unintelligent eyes in this world. All we lack is the required love and willingness to use them.

Inflated inventory

We have claimants who feel that their demand for the

amount of claim is fully justified. But this claim under study is an experienced reality which may prove them wrong.

A poultry farm was damaged by cyclone. The insured reported the loss to underwriters who in turn deputed a surveyor immediately. The surveyor took photographs of the dead birds and submitted his reports assessing the loss of 10,000 full grown birds. On scrutiny it was noticed that less than 500 birds were visibly dead as captured in the photographs. A letter was sent to the insured requesting for clarification of the fact that when less than 500 dead birds were available at the time of survey, how come he had claimed the loss of 10,000 birds. The insured reply that the rest 9,500 birds had been eaten by the dogs.

It is common knowledge that birds are kept in locked cages, hence couldn't have been swept away by cyclonic flood water. Secondly, dogs couldn't enter into the locked cages to eat birds. Thirdly, thousands of dogs were to be available to eat 9,500 birds. In super cyclone, most of the dogs of that area had also died. Even in normal times so many dogs could not be available in a particular area. Thus it was proved beyond doubt that the insured had inflated his inventory. A meeting was arranged with the insured in the presence of the surveyor and the claim was compromised for a very reasonable amount.

Photographs do not tell lies and are more authentic

than human words. How can we claim that man is the ultimate creation of God?

Pay if you can

One insurance office had issued a fire policy with storm, tempest, flood and inundation extension for which extra premium was charged. It so happened that one fine afternoon the underwriters were on a visit to the insured factory wherein a gantry crane was moving on rails. It was working very fine. To the utter dismay of the underwriters a claim for Rs 10 lakh was lodged with the company next morning stating that this gantry crane moved of its own breaking the stoppers, fell down on ground and got damaged. The insured had no machinery breakdown cover. Hence after a brief scrutiny, the office closed the file as no claim.

The insured represented and put lot of pressure on the company to pay the claim insisting that since loss was genuine and why should not they pay. The file was reviewed and the underwriters went into depth about the cause of loss. The incidence had typical story to tell. How the crane had fallen was really beyond anyone's imagination but the claim was still within the scope of policy. The surveyor explained that the gantry crane ran on rails. It had a hanging control cabin. Whenever the job was over, the operator of crane was to put the operating device on gear before disembarking from cabin. Then he was supposed to lock the windows. In this case, the windows were not properly fastened and late in the evening there was thunder storm and heavy downpour of rain. This resulted in water sneaking to the cabin causing short circuit and putting the operating system in neutral. Once operating system was in neutral, the gantry crane started moving of its own.

This seemed to be a reasonable enough argument. Looking into the cause of loss explained by the surveyor, the under writers had called for meteorological report which confirmed occurrence of heavy rain and thunderstorm. The claims team checked up the policy and found that extra premium for storm peril had appropriately been paid. Contrary to the notion that insurance officials are always bent on mindless application of rules, the company settled the claim and in turn earned the goodwill of client. Let it be known to the millions of clients in the world that the insurance comprehensively taken is panacea for all losses and they should remove the wrong notion that non-life insurance companies promise more and deliver less.

CHAPTER 17

Secrets of Making Underwriting Profit

Outsource most of what you are doing and do it yourself all that you have outsourced. During the last five years the PSU non-life insurance companies are struggling in the quicksand of underwriting losses. With each step they take to get out of it, they sink deeper with little hope of reaching the firm land of profit. It is called quicksand for two reasons: one, because of obscene under-pricing of their products. These days under quoting has gone beyond cut-throat competition because there is no throat left to be cut. The underwriters are cutting their own throats in the name of price war by giving more than 90% discount even in loss making business. Two, because there is no serious concern for the management of claims. These two reasons are fatal enough to take the very life out of any non-life insurance company. There is no one-size-fits-all method to bring in magical solution to this gargantuan problem. But the following are some pragmatic practices that could be followed to remain in business with profitability, dignity, and with sound solvency margin.

Supervise the Process of Survey

Not supervising the survey of big claims means creating opportunities for huge leakages. The man is unique creation of God. He is not a being but has the potentiality of perpetually becoming different under different circumstances. Man can resist anything but temptation. A good man can become bad. A competent surveyor may err because to err is human. We have put far too much reliance on the surveyors. They are required to be supervised not after they submit their reports but during survey and preparation of the report. In case of big claims, the survey should be supervised at every stage of claim's progress right from admission of liability, document verification, assessment of claim and disposal of salvage. This could be done by the claims team through constant meetings with both the surveyor and the insured. Nothing should be left to be read and understood after the survey report is issued. It is much easier to prevent a wrong assessment than rectifying it after the report is released.

The survey supervision is more important and more vital than any other activity of the company because a surveyor has enormous scope to use his discretionary authority limitlessly without accountability. But unfortunately very little or no attention is paid to this aspect. Hence there is immense possibility of claims being manipulated. To supervise survey, the team members should be technically sound and be genuinely concerned for timely and judicious settlement. They should analyze, discuss with their peers, superiors and experts from time to time to get the most accurate assessment. Near or total absence of thorough supervision could be the proximate cause of the leakage which in turn becomes a major contributing factor for underwriting losses. A survey report should be read in the process of its making. To read a report after it is issued is like speaking first and thinking later.

In the present system of big claim processing, every official thinks that the other must have read the file. Hence he need not read. But sometimes in reality nobody goes through it. Even if they go through, they would not find the truth. By reading a report they may see the apparent but not the actual. They may get the surveyor's perception of truth, the purity of which depends on his ingenuity and the level of his spiritual and ethical upbringing to accurately reveal the same. Moreover the survey report along with documents of big claims arrive in thousand pages which makes it too repulsive for the officials to open it unless someone is involved from the very beginning.

The PSUs do not have skilled people in the corporate claims cell who are specially trained and exclusively selected to handle big claims. The skeletal department consists of officials who are accidentally posted there just to put up claim files received from Regional Offices to the competent authority for approval. Selecting claim managers is as much vital as selecting operational heads. It is about time to wake up and put all efforts to give a surgical finish to each big claim to restore the health of company's balance sheet. They may entirely outsource any other activity but not claims. What it requires is a small fraction of the determination of Columbus, intuition of Birbal and the courage of Shivaji Maharaj. These are all inherent in us and only need to be activated through sheer passion for the pursuit of excellence. If the PSUs direct most of their energy to meticulous supervision of survey by a team of specially trained and dedicated officials, underwriting losses as an intractable problem will be a thing of the past.

On choosing the right Surveyor

Well begun is half done. The very appointment of a surveyor determines which direction the claim is going to go. Once JRD Tata when asked about the secret of his success. prompt came the reply "I choose the right man for the right job and then forget about it." Do PSUs do that? First the officials must know who is right. To know that they must be right first. Nothing remains a secret in insurance industry. Everyone knows who is what and the truth is spoken in half whispers and every one whispers to everyone because that is our national character. In the process the truth remains a safe secret in the knowledge of every one. The appointment of the surveyor reflects the credibility of the insurance official who appoints him. Some private companies do not appoint another surveyor for re-inspection in motor claim saying that they have full trust in the surveyor they are appointing.

The formalities of appointing a surveyor for a big claim many times takes a disappointing five days length. As per the statement of a PSU branch manager, the big claim intimation travels from the branch office to the divisional office, finally lands in the head office after a brief halt at regional office. The claims department at HO puts up a note to the competent authority and precious five days are lost in the process and one third of the survey fee is paid to a preliminary surveyor unnecessarily. The whole thing could be avoided if the appointment is done over phone in minutes and is formalized afterwards.

Immediate Team Visit to the Site of Claim: A Must

If the travel records of the corporate officials are analyzed, it would reveal that no or negligible number of tours must have been undertaken to the site of claim for getting first hand information and initiating claim minimization processes. This means that the big claims are entirely left to the whims and fancies of the surveyors which could be one of the most important factors of soaring claim ratio .

Here is a real life example of what happens if the site of claim is not visited by the insurance officials. The engine room of a ship was damaged by fire and was dry docked in a foreign land for repair. An estimate of Rs.18 crore was received by the underwriters in India. An overseas loss adjuster was appointed. A fortnight after, a revised estimate of Rs.35 crore was received. Since neither the protest was lodged nor a visit to the site of repair was made, the repairers re-revised the estimate to Rs.75 crore and then further to Rs.105 crore. And the claim finally was assessed for Rs. 78 crore and as usual got settled on the strength of the survey report. A visit to the site of repair by the underwriters accompanied by an expert would have cost the company a few lakh but certainly would have saved many a crore. The insurance companies are the trustees of people who give their money with trust to be best managed and not to be squandered away.

Very recently there was a huge fire loss in Byculla, Mumbai. The concerned private insurance company was informed that estimate of loss would be about Rs.50 crore.Within hours the claims Head,   ,the marketing Head and the Head of risk management along with the surveyor were at the site. After their physical inspection, instantly the estimate came down to Rs.10 lakh. This small episode reveals their team spirit, transparency, concern and pro-active approach to management of claims in epic proportion. It is expected that the PSUs will rise to this level of handling claims.

Fast, fair and friendly settlement

An iron ore processing unit at mines site was severely damaged by mud slide following heavy rains. And the plant and machineries were buried under 20 feet of mud. It was insured with a private sector company (the only company which makes underwriting profit every year) under fire policy on replacement value basis. The Claims Head after getting the intimation, rushed a local surveyor to the site and got the ILA (Immediate Loss Advice) that read insured's estimate of loss as Rs.

63 crore and surveyor's estimate as Rs. 35 crore. The claim head rushed to the site along with his team with the motto "arise, awake and sleep not till the claim is settled". And soon after, the final surveyor joined them. Damaged machineries were jointly inspected, purchase papers were asked for and scrutinized in the presence of the insurance officials. After one more meeting, it was decided to settle the claim on market value basis since it came to light that the unit was heavily under- insured. The clients were politely explained about it in the meeting. The claim was settled within 21 days after the surveyor submitted his report for Rs. 18 crore. The Insured was pleased. The underwriters were relieved of their liability quickly and followed up recovery from the reinsurers. If it were a PSU insurance company, the whole thing probably would have been left to the surveyor and apart from inordinate delay, the assessment would have solely depended on the credibility of the surveyor.

A private company has settled the toughest of big claims in record 29 days time. The PSUs should have definite time limit from the date of loss till settlement and implement the same through constant monitoring because delay is a huge catalyst for precipitating exaggerated assessment. Paying out claims in fair and equitable manner helps stabilizing profit for the Company and enhances confidence of the customer in insurance mechanism.

Faster Repudiation of no Claim

A claim has a life cycle- birth, childhood, youth and old age. The older it is, the more painful it is to the underwriters. Like a festering wound, the quicker it is treated and cured, better is the relief. Especially if it is a no claim, it should be communicated to the Insured in writing within days citing the valid reason thereof, otherwise the expectations of the insured will increase with passing of time and after a long period of waiting, rejection may ignite the smouldering anger of delay into flames of litigation.

A fertilizer plant owner having IR policy with MLOP extension intimated the underwriters that the plant was being shut down for maintenance. Four weeks after, they discovered during dismantling some damaged reformer tubes. A senior surveyor was rushed to the site and he informed both the Insured and underwriters in writing that the claim was not payable because the tubes had outlived their life, were overdue for replacement and it was a clear case of wear and tear. The insured had a meeting with the underwriters and both agreed to appoint a fertilizer expert for opinion and his opinion was the same as that of the surveyor. The overseas repairers had the same opinion. The laboratory test had the same opinion. Thus the underwriters sent a no claim letter but for reasons best known to them, gave an option to the insured to discuss the matter in another meeting if they so desired. In the meeting it was mysteriously agreed that the surveyor was to offer the matter a re-look. The surveyor suddenly took a u-turn and gave an opposite version of his earlier report saying that the material damage claim was payable and assessed a huge amount of loss toward LOP claim.

This may sound unusual but true. In the mean time six years have elapsed. The matter is yet to be decided. In non-life insurance, the exposure is so huge and the premium is so little that any prudent underwriter could ill- afford the careless handling of such claims.

Time to form Claims Management Team

Jonathan Swift has said " Vision is the art of seeing things invisible to others." As discussed earlier a team of intelligent, courageous and dedicated officials with established credibility and professional ingenuity should be selected to handle big claims. Here credibility means that they should have sound technical knowledge, unquestionable integrity and the courage to take the right decision: the kind of courage that cannot be intimidated by pressure. Finally they should have love for this job. Once there is a big claim, they should rise to the occasion and be committed till they see the last of the claim. This is possible. No prizes for guessing who is the private sector player who could do it: the company that has notched a respectable combined ratio of 94.01% especially at times when the loss ratio of the rest of the industry is shooting through the roof. Thankfully, some of the PSU regional offices can boast of such record.

Time to spend quality time on Claims

Unlike money, time cannot be arithmetically calculated how much is spent on what. But perceptually about 30% of time is spent on HR related issues like conducting written test and interviews for promotion, conducting training programme for employees to face such tests which have no relevance to company's day-to-day operation and finalizing postings after promotion. Employees in turn take long leave to prepare for such examination because efficiency in the exam matters more than dedication at workplace. In the process the work suffers and dedicated workers suffer too. Frankly speaking, industry has never been benefited by such cumbersome process. This is simply much ado about nothing. Had it been otherwise, the balance sheets would not have been what it is. It is time to take practical steps of righting to-day's wrongs. This is a sheer waste of time. No harm following LIC method and saving such huge waste of time for productive activity.

Again, 10% of their time is spent on IT related issues.

Some server problem here, some modification there, some repair somewhere else is everyday affair. At times, it appears that technology is more time-consuming than time-saving. It begins with opening the mail box which is often crowded with irrelevant but exciting mails. In earlier times the corporate executives were frequently talking to the regional and divisional- in-charges and thereby establishing personal contacts and getting the issues sorted out instantly. These days everything is through e- mail. The casualty: personal contact.

Unknowingly 15% time is devoted to quarterly accounts closing which refuses to close more often than not and the blame falls on IT and technical departments. Meetings follow meetings till the next quarter is due. Grievance, estate and establishment, ministry compliance, audit, official language implementation, vigilance, investment, reinsurance, underwriting and IRDA issues claim 35% of the time. These functions are important but claims management is the most important of all. Only less than 10% of the time is devoted to claims and that too mostly in the late afternoons. Public Sector companies discuss claims only at the time of settlement in their offices when it is too late and precious little could be done to repair any damage. While private sector companies discuss pro-actively at the time of occurrence at the site and continue seamless discussion till the claim is settled judiciously. Claims need cool mind and quality time. Let the day begin with discussion on claims and end with some settlement. What is required at this stage is the change of mindset and concern for reducing underwriting losses. While premium income keeps carrying the burden of potential claims and investment return is earned by deploying and risking capital, prevention of leakages through claim supervision generates pure profit only through deployment of wisdom and professional skill-the human capital that unwittingly remains unutilized. No other activity in the entire practices of non-life insurance can generate such risk-free profit for the company. Hence by all means it deserves more attention and always.

Time to restrict MB and MLOP under IAR Policy

Covering machineries without age limit and extending MLOP cover is suicidal because it amounts to insuring a predictable loss and not an unpredictable risk. More than 30 years old machineries with many hospitalization records bound to break down more often than not and the PSUs cover the same and at the rate which is less than 10% of the old rate: the rate at which the underwriters earlier were covering machineries not more than 5 years old. What is more ridiculous is that even with 900% claim ratio, companies are fighting with each other to renew the said policies with further competitive rates. Time is ripe enough to de- risk the exposure to such age old machineries to bail out their companies from troubling conditions. Motto should not be volume based but value focused.

Extending MLOP to suppliers' premises is another loss breeding proposition. If it cannot be avoided, a wider deductible is an alternative option to reduce the intensity of such claims. The underwriting department should be constantly in touch with claims department to review such portfolio prudently before taking any renewal decision.

Direct Claim Settlement

'Direct claim settlement because relationships do not have space for Third Parties' Thus goes the million dollar slogan of a private sector Health Insurance Company which has the wisdom to realize that Third Party is not a bridge but a barrier in claim settlement. Let accounts of the company be outsourced .Let compilation of statistics be outsourced but not health claims settlement, a practice which most certainly alienates the customers from the underwriters and deprives the latter of having the experience of control on the claims outgo. Unless someone handles claims, he can never be a good underwriter. Firsthand information from claims is the raw material from which finished product of underwriting is made. The irony is that the companies pay a part of their premium to get deprived of these opportunities. Moreover many wrong claim settlements may go unnoticed Who has the time, man power and expertise to find them? But certainly it adds quietly to the woes of underwriting losses.

Regular Workshop and Training on Claims

It is a fact admitted universally that leakages in claims are to the tune of 20% which if translated into amount would be more than thousand crore for each company. During last one decade there has hardly been any brain- storming session on handling big claims. Non-life insurance subjects are vast and the claims are vastly complicated in nature. Sharing of information is vital to update one's knowledge and sharpen one's skill. It is only possible through knowing what is happening where. Regular seminars and more frequent workshops on claims involving industry experts from the better managed private sectors would most certainly enhance the capability of the PSUs.

Business Ethics and Underwriting

A Japanese couple invited another couple to their home for drinks, dinner and overnight stay. The guest couple enjoyed the hospitality and while taking leave the morning next, they profusely thanked the hosts for all the trouble they had taken. But the hosts quickly interrupted and said, rather we should thank you to have shared our mosquitoes. It does not help in any manner to snatch each other's mosquitoes generating business. Its effect is too obvious to go unnoticed. The compulsory quota share has been dropped down by the GIC Re from 20% to 5% and further reduction is contemplated. Many last treaty renewals were in trouble. Even the customer friendly surplus treaty re-insures have started pushing for the per location and per event limit.

Going blindly after market share means taking too much risk. Height and size do not matter. What matters is good health. The recent cautionary instructions from the ministry to exercise categorical discipline in health insurance underwriting is praise worthy. The PSUs need to have the same business discipline in other portfolios until IRDA takes a stimulus from the ministry and imposes minimum rates to redirect the industry back to business ethics. "The greatness of living lies not in never falling but in rising every time we fall." It is time for the PSUs to awake. If they choose to do so, it would mean taking a giant leap in the right direction.

CHAPTER 18

Rising Claim Ratio and Prevention

Even when seeing is not believing, how come
we believe without seeing.
- Edmund Burke

Edmund Burke the famous British historian, was assigned to write the history of the world from its origin. He had already spent fifty years of his life writing a thousand pages. One evening, on hearing some noise near his house he came out and saw a man lying dead There was a huge gathering of people. Someone was saying that he committed suicide, someone else said he had been murdered, the third emphasized that it was just an accidental death and the fourth proclaimed that he had a fatal heart attack. Edmund Burke could not believe it. "The dead man is lying before me and there are four opinions and I am writing a book about a thousand years of past events which I have not seen myself and trying to prove that it is factual." He went back to his study and burnt those thousand pages. Even when seeing is not believing, how come we believe without seeing.

The harsh fact is that every so often insurance officials of Public Sector Insurance Companies in India do not visit the site of claim and when they visit, the result is amazing: claims are settled quickly and assessments are done judiciously. Here are some claims which will speak volumes on the subjects.

Labour and the Reward

A shrimp processing plant in Andhra Pradesh was severely affected by a cyclone in October 1996. Huge stocks of shrimp pertaining to three different firms were stored in the refrigeration unit of the plant. The entire unit got affected due to inundation. Shivam Sea Foods, one of the firms had insured its stock with Oriental Insurance Company. Responding to the intimation for a total loss of Rs.100 lakh, Dr.Satyanarayan, Divisional Manager visited the processing plant and observed with intelligence that a huge quantity of unaffected stock would deteriorate due to interruption in supply of electricity to the plant as a result of the cyclone. The prudent Divisional Manager convinced the insured to shift unaffected stock stored above water level to another plant situated seven kilometers away where power was available. Despite the fact that there was two feet of water logging in the plant site, Dr. Satyanarayan spent the whole day participating in shifting of the stock. His hard labour did not go in vain as the loss was brought down to Rs. 40 lakh, thereby saving the insurance company a sum of Rs. 60 lakh. Stocks pertaining to the other two firms stored in the same plant insured with other insurance companies were assessed on total loss basis by the respective surveyors since none of their officials either visited the site or were concerned about the loss minimisation.

Trustworthiness

Jai Bharat Bullion reported a claim for 900 kg of silver alleged to have been washed away in flood water in its liquid form. The claim management team visited the unit along with a prudent surveyor. The unit had about 15 workers present round the clock in the factory premises because they had their accommodation adjacent to the shop floor itself. On inspection it was found that the processing unit had only two vessels containing silver liquid which had the capacity only to contain 40 kg of liquid silver each and remain half filled at any given time.

The team asked from which of his clients 900 kg of bullion came from, the proof thereof, relevant claim papers of such clients lodging their claim with the insured and asking for compensation. Moreover, it was clearly evident that the unit had a first floor accommodation and the liquid silver could easily have been carried to the first floor along with the container or in small containers as the flood water came gradually and not suddenly. On enquiry by the claim management team, the insured could not provide any information and chose to remain taciturn and evasive on the source from which he had received 900 kg. of bullion. The insured had already been paid a claim for the loss of 790 kg of silver having been washed away in the previous flood from the same underwriters. The team asked for details of payments that he had made to his customers to whom he had reimbursed the amount of the previous claim which he could not and realizing that he was heading for trouble he did not take further interest in the second claim. As a result, the claim was treated as no claim and the insured was given the reason thereof. This clearly demonstrates the falsity on the part of the insured. However, insurer's timely intervention proved to be effective in preventing such an act of manipulation for the second time.

Stock held in trust claims are payable only when the customers of the insured have preferred their claims on him, which need further investigation to confirm its authenticity. The unit has the capacity to process maximum of 80 kg of silver at any given point of time. Hence it was not prudent to consider such big volumes without verifying the details of processing. Such dark anomalies can only be brought to light only by visiting the site of claim and putting one's intelligence at work.

Getting into the heart of the matter

A leading Pharmacy Company certified by the Govt. of USA, having very strict quality control measures, reported a claim for damage to stock of imported raw materials and packing materials due to flood water. The Insured estimated the loss for Rs. 15 crore and wanted total loss settlement since the drums containing the stock were totally submerged in flood water and hence could not be salvaged.

On receipt of claim intimation the Claim Management Team rushed to insured's plant. During inspection it was noticed that raw materials were very expensive and highly sensitive to moisture and hence were stored in a cold chamber under controlled temperature. Water had entered into the cold chamber and drums containing raw material were submerged in the water for some time. Special Cold chamber machineries too stopped functioning for some time. The Insured had apprehensions that a substantial stock of raw material might have got damaged both due to drums coming in contact with water and non-functionality of cold chamber machinery for some time. The insured was in no frame of mind to continue talk on salvaging the stock since the raw materials were meant for manufacturing of life-saving drugs.

Before the situation got toxic, the Insurance officials politely persuaded the insured to get the samples of raw materials tested in the lab and get all parameters checked. On testing it was found intact in all respects since the drums were water proof. Inspired by the positive results of the sample test, 100% of the affected stock was tested and was found absolutely unaffected by the flood.

Finally, the entire stock of raw material was accepted by the insured as there was no trace of any deterioration found in the quality. The claim was restricted to the damaged packing materials only for Rs. 15 lakh instead of Rs.15 crore as claimed. It was a great relief for the insurance company from an impossible situation but not without the insurance officials breaking into sweat.

Application of Simple Common Sense

The insured had claimed that four armed men came to the construction site at 1.00 am and two of them confined the security staff in the wash room. The rest two armed men loaded 15 metric tonnes of steel into the truck and sped away at 2.00 am. The intelligent claims manager tore into the illogical survey report and repudiated the claim writing to the insured that it was not possible for two men to load 15 metric tonnes of steel in just one hour under such tense circumstances. The matter went to the Court after the underwriters rejected the claim but the honorable judge was convinced in favour of the insurance company and the matter was finally closed.

A Step in the right direction

The man who decides how much to be paid is more respectful than the one who is authorised to pay the claim. Thus the respectability and the reputation of PSU companies have been hijacked by lawyers, surveyors and third party administrators with remarkable ease. Like the absent minded professor who after arriving at the destination station handed over his purse to porter to carry and himself carried his luggage to the taxi stand. The passion to participate in the details of claim management by Public Sector Insurance Company officials is not in their blood. Hence, more often than not, their business results go into a tailspin. If such nightmarish practices of leaving claims to third parties continues, the companies will not be able to arrest the rising underwriting deficit.

The PSUs should junk the traditional method of sending surveyors alone for the assessment of loss and must have their claim management team on the site to supervise the assessment of loss. This way consumer connect can also be reinforced. They must embrace reforms to rein in underwriting deficits and not fall far too behind the private sectors in minimising losses. The PSUs need to change majorly if they have to improve claim management efficiency to firewall their balance sheets from the flames of crisis. They need to realise this basic truth and ensure its implementation in letter and spirit.

There is no perfect way to handle claims since each claim demands a customised approach and application of intelligence and this is only possible if the Claim Managers are present at the site of claim and take decisions on seeing things rather than on reading reports. A veteran observer of the industry has said it right – if the general insurance PSUs in India want to stay in business, they should outsource what they themselves are doing at present like HR, accounting, audit, statistics and let themselves do what they have outsourced like property claims, medi-claim and TP claims. When companies are sinking in worries that in future they might not have enough investment income to pay for the claimant, how long can they afford to stay away from the site of claim which holds both the lock and key to claim management?

CHAPTER 19

True Claims that are Stranger than Fiction

With coming of the open market, the severe cut throat competition as no throat left to be cut in further rate cutting. Despite having the principle of risk based underwriting in the back of their minds, the underwriters have involuntarily allowed themselves to be the victims of such unethical practices. Under such circumstances, to allow a fraudulent claim or an inflated amount of loss to be paid to a dishonest customer would amount to not only twice abusing the insurance system but giving a coup de grace to company's own balance sheet. To conduct an instant on-site investigation by quality and capable claim managers will prevent the fraudsters from exploiting the system. It is easier to find signs of fraud on claim

site than by going through the survey report with a
fine-tooth comb.

Uncovering the Truth

Fire claim in edible oil mill was reported at Amritnagar
divisional office. Since the estimated amount was big,
the regional office at Chandinagar deputed a surveyor
who quietly landed at the site of claim without
the knowledge of the divisional office, inspected
the damaged mill, collected relevant papers and
submitted his report assessing the loss for an amount
of Rs.60 lakh directly to the regional office. The
prudent divisional manager with an unquestionable
established credibility objected to the whole process
and wanted to have the claim site visited jointly with
the surveyor. The report had mentioned short circuit
as the cause and the fire had originated and spread
from the control panel. On inspection it was found
that there was no connecting medium to carry fire
from the control panel to different sections of mill
since there were considerable empty spaces between
them. Suspicion grew stronger since fire had occurred
here and there and was not continuous spread from
the source origin.

The divisional office team had the salvage sample
officially collected from the floors of different sections
for lab test with consent of the insured who needed

persuasion to give his consent. The report from the government lab confirmed that the salvage contained chemical oil and not edible oil spill. Hence it was a clear case of arson, the basis on which the claim was politely repudiated. Further dig in the matter revealed that the insured's business was not doing well and the mill was closed for a considerable length of time. The incident of fire was to exploit insurance to compensate the loss of business. The insured reconciled to the truth and did not protest against the repudiation of claim. But many such claims get paid.

The local transit fraud

A marine transit claim for theft of full truck load of export quality Basmati rice from the Nectar City to Kandla port was recommended by branch office to divisional office for approval. All the documents required were furnished. Hence the official in the division recommended to the divisional manager for approval. On scrutiny the divisional manager felt that although all documents for Basmati rice transit claim are in order yet why should not we enquire about the claim of the truck which was also stolen.

Branch office wrote to insured and quick reply came that the divisional manager was asking unnecessary queries, since the truck is not insured with the same company. But the divisional manager remained firm and asked for at least a copy of FIR lodged with police for theft of truck. This resulted in threats to the divisional manager and complaint to his higher authorities for deliberate delay and asking for money. The regional manager on scrutiny of file himself agreed with the genuine queries of his junior colleague. Now no alternative remained with claimants but to supply a copy of FIR lodged with police for theft of the truck. In the meantime office deputed an investigator for tracing the route of the truck. He informed that upto border of the neighbouring city he did not find any entry of this truck number at any of the toll gates. Then he was asked to get the RC of the truck verified from RTA. To every one's utter surprise the RC was issued for a scooter and not for the truck.

Ultimately the office received the copy of the Final Investigation Report for theft of truck issued by SSP of the district. The office wrote to the SSP enclosing reports of the investigator. On this, SSP in writing quashed the FIR and sent a copy to the divisional office also.

The engine and chassis number of the so called truck was already recorded in the claim document. Now the office wrote to the the manufacturers as to which dealer they have supplied the truck manufactured with that engine and chassis numbers. Reply came that they had never manufactured a truck with those numbers at any of its plants. Based on these facts the claim was repudiated with a politely speaking repudiation letter addressed to insured. The insured approached many forums but his claim was rejected by one and all with confirmations that company was absolutely right.

Documentary fraud in overseas consignments

Ignorance is not always bliss. Certainly not in marine insurance. Non- vessel Operating Common Carrier is "carrier to the shipper," and "shipper to the carrier". Initially they issue their own bill of lading to be immediately followed by a master bill of lading from the shipping company. In the case under discussion Hiralal, the Insured sent consignment of rugs to Atlanta Rugs in USA, and insured it with a PSU insurance company under ICC (A) cover. The consignment was handed over to the shipping agent who issued NVOCC (non-vessel operating common carrier) bill of lading. Consignors endorsed this B/L and other original documents in favor of their Bankers in Mumbai who discounted the bill and in turn forwarded original documents to Sun Trust Bank, Atlanta, for "collection" by endorsing the original documents in their favor.
But the buyer neither turned up to collect original documents from the Sun Trust within time limit of 90 days nor The Sun Trust returned the documents to the Bankers in Mumbai to deal with the same at latter's end. The consignors were informed accordingly. The

consignor lodged a claim with the insurance company. The claims agent of the underwriters investigated and submitted his report. The consignors were informed that the buyers had apparently taken delivery of the consignment by producing Master B/L clandestinely sent to them by theNVOCC. Hence the claim was repudiated.

Hiralal went into litigation at National Forum. The Commission had observed that the policy covered "all risks of loss". Since the original documents of title were not taken by the buyers and were returned to the Indian banker by the Sun Trust Bank, the delivery could not be taken and there was no evidence about the fate of the shipments, hence it is a "loss" and insurers had to indemnity the said loss.

The underwriters approached Honourable Supreme Court in appeal. The Court observed that no Master B/L was obtained and submitted by consignor along with documents of title. No prudent consignor will do this. The policy covers loss due to insured perils occurring during the journey. There was no attempt by Sun Trust Bank or buyer to approach the carrier to obtain delivery. Had delivery been refused, this would have meant that goods were lost during transit The shipping agent colluded with the buyers by directly sending him master B/L resulting thereby clandestine delivery of the consignment. It is not a loss of consignment. The claimant should prove the actual loss of consignment. The insurers were right in rejecting the claim.

Where there is will

There is a way. It is true in management of claims. SBI General received many stock claims from coconut traders in 2012 Cyclone in Andhra Pradesh. Most of the claimants transact in cash while purchasing from farmers and selling to retailers. Thus bank statements could not be available to form the basis of assessment of loss. Physical inspection of the site did not give accuracy of stocks as all are stored in open areas and only about 25% were either stored in godowns or under the shades. Surveyors were not in a position to ascertain the loss. Volumetric analysis could not be applied as the storage was in open farm spreading over number of acres. Surveyors were asked to take the physical inventory of the existing stocks just after the loss and record it with acknowledgement of the insured. They expressed their inability to assess the loss in the absence of proper books confirming the transactions and some surveyors were apprehensive that the books were prepared after the loss showing the existence of huge stocks before the cyclone .It had become difficult to assess the actual stocks lost.

The business did not fall under MODVAT. It did not fall under CST. The insurance company needed a breakthrough in the claims. The claim officer accompanied surveyors to the affected area. While speaking to some of the farmers he could grab upon a piece of information that all merchants have to pay 1% to 2% cess to AMC (Agriculture market committee) depending on the quality of the coconut on monthly basis and it was mandatory. With a sigh of relief the officer went to agriculture market committee office and got it confirmed. He asked for cess receipts and on that basis he could work out the stocks of the farmer just before the cyclone and assessed the loss after deducting the stock saved and thanked the farmer who gave such information which could save the SBI General from paying inflated amount of claim. It is said "If you have the earnest desire to do a good thing , the whole existence will conspire with you in getting it done."

Few words in the end

The society is having the incorrect perception that the insurance companies will do whatever they can to avoid paying a claim. This is certainly not true but that is the impression of the many. Therefore insurance officials should be trained and be adequately equipped with external know-how that is knowledge, internal expertise that is intelligence and commitment to pay a genuine claim quickly and fraudulent claim judiciously. Money invested on training officials in preventing fraud will reap great harvest of benefit for the Company. Otherwise overlooking an insurance fraud will encourage the creation of further fraud and will result in contamination of insurance brand.

CHAPTER 20

Inflated Assessment and Consequences

Challenging an assessment of claim is no luxury. Once challenged, the matter heads for controversy. But the plus side of the controversy is that company saves money and the surveyor gets a "shake up" of his conscience. To get a claim reduced after the survey report has been issued is like getting back life from the jaws of death. However, brave and intelligent officers, sufficiently equipped with wisdom of experience, do it by risking their peace of mind and sometimes incurring the wrath of all concerned. These are the people who look deep into the heart of things to see their true nature and have the skill to convince the insured about the authenticity of the matter. It almost seems like they are born just to do that. Here are some sachet versions of huge anomalies which if go unnoticed, can bring slow and sure ruin to the company's balance sheet.

Insured's Bravery, Insurer's Misery

Flood water flows, stays and ebbs out. The think tank in automobile engineering is of the opinion that the flood water can enter the engine either through the exhaust pipe or through the air pipe. These two vital parts meet the engine at more than two feet height. If assessment of flood loss to the engine where the water level is less than this, think it over. The Pundits further emphasize that when a car gets affected by flood water, the parts inside the engine do not get damaged unless it is "for ce-started" by dragging from the front or by pushing from behind. Every car owner needs to know that damage of engine parts due to "force-starting" is not payable under the insurance policy because such damage is neither accidental and nor by external means. And such parts can never be damaged if the vehicle is simply towed to the garage without force-starting, a fact too important to be ignorant about. Therefore inflated assessment is a constant presence in such claims. Imagine the number of cars affected in Mumbai flood and such claims paid which could have been avoided.

Due to such "force-starting" of the vehicles, the parts

like pistons get buckled up, engine walls get damaged, piston rings and connecting rod get impacted. The assessment of repair and replacement of such parts which at times becomes many times more than the actual indemnity of cleaning charges of the engine is not payable but unfortunately gets paid.The motor surveyors' lackadaisical approach to the policy exclusions and the claim managers' reckless indifference to technical aspects of the engine, have short-circuited the very principle on which premium pricing is transmitted; and the motor portfolio is bound to skid on such uneven assessments and drag down the company's balance-sheet to the path of ruin. It is immensely significant for all of us both to keep it in mind and enlighten the customers.

Offending the Principle of Indemnity

A major fire destroyed the electronic goods and spares but the floors where records of accounts were maintained remained unaffected.The Insured maintained accounts and inventory in the IT-based tally system. The loss reported was INR.184 lakh (US$396,000) and the insurers promptly visited the spot along with the surveyors.

The surveyors assessed the loss for INR.135 lakh and submitted their report promptly recommending on account payment of INR.100 lakh. The loss was more due to the spray of water by fire brigade than by the spread of fire. The surveyors had allowed the insured to get the water- damaged spares tested from a lab situated in Bangalore even when the location of the risk was in Chennai. But they made no mention of the obsolete stocks much to the discomfort of the underwriters. As the fire had not spread to the accounts sections, the claim managers called for all the documents pertaining to the imports and found that many of such items were five to ten years old and had remained unsold for more than five years.

Market investigation revealed that the spares were of no use due to widespread adoption of the digital technology. Obviously the insured did not allow the underwriters to check the records generated using IT based Tally package. This led to suspicion over the authenticity of the transaction.

Truth sometimes needs a nasty way of coming out. A decision to send the repudiation letter citing policy conditions was taken by the underwriters. The insured could sense the proposed repudiation and quickly came forward for negotiation. Supported by strong evidence, the insurance company explained the logic of not allowing the claim of obsolete goods and deducting the profit element from the calculation. In the process the amount got scaled down from INR.134 lakh to INR.57 lakh. The insured finally agreed for the same.To avoid any complication in future, the underwriters got a revised claim form filled in which generated a revised survey report for INR.57 lakh. The insured appreciated the gesture of quick settlement and continued placing all his business with this company.

Unveiling the Secrets of Underinsurance

A wholesaler had a stock of medicine in his godown and it was severely affected by the devastating flood of Mumbai on 25th July 2005. The insured claimed for total sum insured of Rs..6 crore. The claim was undoubtedly genuine and the surveyor assessed the loss for Rs.4 crore and submitted his report.

The stock was financed by a bank and the surveyor had taken into account the stock statement submitted by the insured to the bank for the month of June for the assessment of loss. It was pointed out that the sum insured was Rs.6 crore only and stock statement was for Rs.10 crore and hence there was underinsurance of 40% which the surveyor had not applied in his assessment.It quickly set off a raging debated over the issue. The surveyor defended by saying that the stock worth of Rs.4 crore was returned by the insured to the manufacturer on 12, 13 and 14 of July 2005. The underwriters asked for the LR numbers and the dates of the relevant dispatches. The surveyors replied that these stocks were returned through auto rickshaws.

His rebuttal was not effective. The underwriters dismissed it as a pack of lies.

The foundation of a lie always remains brittle and shaky and at the end the truth always prevails. A shadow of lie can dim the illumination of truth only temporarily. The stock statement for July submitted by the insured on 18th of August was also for Rs.10 crore. Since the flood occurred on 25th July and there was no movement of stock for several days after the flood, it was confirmed that the stock at the material time of flood wasRs.10 crore. Moreover annual reports read that the closing stock on 31st March 2004 was Rs.14 crore. Similarly, the closing stock on 31st March 2005 was Rs.12 crore. Therefore, as per the insured's own record, the godown consistently had Rs.10 crore of stock. Such strong evidence put the surveyor squarely in the dock of accounting scrutiny. He relaxed his stand and applied 40% under insurance which the insured who was considerate and undemanding, accepted towards full and final settlement.

Navigating Step by Step

A stock of synthetic yarn was affected by storm and flood. It was insured for Rs.66 lakh and the surveyor submitted his report for Rs.44 lakh. The underwriters were uncomfortable because the damaged stocks had been removed immediately to another godown of safety before they visited the site.

The matter was referred to the claim manager on the assumption that the insured had claimed more and the surveyor had not assessed judiciously. On study of the report, it was found that surveyor had quoted from the insured's claim intimation letter stating that there was one and half feet of flood water around the godown. Hence, water had entered the premises and damaged the stock. The photographs of the compound showed that

one had to climb six steps from ground level to reach the floor of the godown. The height of six steps would be a minimum of three feet. Hence, the possibility of flood water reaching such heights and damaging the stocks was remote as per the law of nature and the surveyor agreed to the fact without much resistance.

Then came the possibility of damage due to collapse of the roof. It was seen from the photographs that only 20% of the roof had collapsed from one side allowing the rain water to fall on the 20% stock amounting to Rs.13 Lakh only. Tiles of the collapsed roof were not heavy enough to tear into the cones. Since cones were first wrapped in the waterproof polythene and again each dozen cones were packed in large polythene bags, the chances of rain water entering the entire 20% of the stock was again a remote possibility. Hence, step by step, the logical structure of calculation was established and the claim was revised down to Rs.9 lakh. When informed, the insured sounded upset for a while but was convinced by the overwhelming evidence.

Visiting the site of Claim is a Stich in Time

A claim for the loss of beer and wine due to fllod water was reported to a PSU Insurance Company. As usual in a very casual response a surveyor was deputed without a team of official the site of claim as is done in a private sector.The learned surveyor bravely assessed the loss for Rs.1Crore 35lakh. His contention was that since the bottles of wine and beer were under water for more than two hours, the contents were not worthy of consumption.There were 42 panchanamas from excise department stating that the materials had been destroyed as per the order passed by the State Excise Department.In the aforesaid order there was also a stipulation for videographing the destruction process.The total number of bottles claimed to have been destroyed for which assessment had been done were 170000.No videography was done.Instead the ccTV recordings of a few days had been submitted by the Insured.The surveyor was defiant and non-cooperative.Prompted by his wisdom he explained that since a Government department had given destruction panchnama, there was no necessity of videography or other evidences.

Claim was repudiated.citing the reason that how werethere were no evidences how the affected bottles were disposed of.As per ccTVrecording, the bottles were being emptied one by one in a bucket. In twenty minutes only two bottles have been emptied.Imagine how much time it would take to empty 170000 bottles. No where the empty bottles could be found in eyes of the camera. Sometimes the insured said bottles were thrown in the dustbin,and some other time he said that the bottles were sold as scrap.

But it was too little and too late that could make a difference.The insured has gone to Consumer Forum.A visit to the site by a team of competent officials and appointing a prudent surveyor could have saved a lot of time and ensured right assessment saving a huge amount of public money.If we sort out a problem immediately, it is sure to save a lot of extra work later. The problem   certainly becomes bigger and bigger with passing of time.A stich in time saves ni

Pulse of the Matter

Such claims become incredibly complex. Such situations generate considerable tension, lead to ugly confrontations and hence need to be handled gently with patience and forgiveness.

Very often the managers face anxious moments and fight losing battles. Yet, they take salutary steps and fight with insight to bring out the truth in its pristine form and the lost battles are won with the weapons of conviction. Our balance sheets have become a bottomless pit. We are heavily depending on the investment income to fill up the void. Investment income can take us so far and no further. Galileo has rightly said: "All truths are easy to understand once they are discovered; the point is to discover them."

CHAPTER 21

Insurance Lessons from Ramayan and Mahabharat

King Dasharath and Underwriting

Kaikeyi was the most favourite Queen of King Dasharatha. She used to accompany king to every battle he fought. She too fought side by side. If any poisonous arrow of the enemy would pierce into the body of the king Dasarath, she would pull out the arrow and suck out poisonous blood from his wound, arrange for the cure and make it healthy again. In one of such battles, Dasaratha's chariot went out of control because bolt of one of the wheels slipped out and the wheel was about to disengage when a brave and daredevil Kaikeyi inserted her thumb in the hole of the bolt and made the chariot operational.And the battle was won. Dasharath was overwhelmed with feelings of thankfulness and appreciation for queen Kaikeyi ,and said ' I am so grateful. You ask any wish any time, it will be fulfilled. It is my promise.' It is said by the wise that do not take any big decision either in a hurry or when filled with uncontrollable emotions of ecstasy or agony without analyzing the consequence it may have in future. In such situations man is very low in his capacity for rational thought and hence the decisions taken may not be in conformity with established procedure. 'By saying ask anything any time' King Dasaratha remained vulnerable to unlimited time and limitless wish. Kaikeyi asked Ramachandra to quit and go to forest for fourteen years and her son Bharat be crowned as the King of Ajyodhya, an act that had disastrous consequences. It was a kind of careless underwriting or verbal commitment on the part of King Dasharatha for a promise that ruined his kingdom and caused death to his own life.

Dasharatha Syndrome in Twin Towers Insurance

Pattern of Dasharatha symptoms are indicative of some similarity in underwriting of Twin Towers. On July 24,2001,Mr.Silverstein purchased the Twin Towers for $ 3.2 billion and insured both the towers on First Loss basis from In simple language the Insured and the Underwriters assumed that under any circumstances both the towers cannot be destroyed simultaneously. Therefore only one tower was insured for $3.2 billion on the condition that if one tower gets damaged by a peril, from the indemnity amount which the insurer is liable to pay the amount of premium will be automatically deducted and the second one will deem to be insured from the same moment. First aircraft crashed on one Tower at 8.45 AM and the second one crashed on the other after 18 minutes at 9.03 AM.

Since Duration Clause was not incorporated in the policy document, the Insured, Silverstein Properties made two claims of $3.2 billion each. The underwriters advocated it as one claim since there was only eighteen minutes difference between two occurrences. The case went to the court and series of court decisions finally determined that a maximum of $4.55 billion was payable. If the underwriters would have put Twenty-Four-Hours-Duration Clause stating that all the claims occurring during a period of twenty four hours will be treated as one claim, the liability of the underwriters would have limited to Sum Insured of $3.2 billion only.

Laxman Rekha and Jewelers' Block Insurance

Since Lord Rama who went on chasing the illusory golden dear did not return in expected time, thinking that Rama might have been in danger, Sita requested Lxman to go in search of Rama. Laxman hesitatingly agreed but drew three lines around the ashram cottage informing Sita not to come out beyond those lines under any circumstances. Ravan came in disguise of a hermit and asked for alms. A gullible Sita was persuaded to come beyond the lines and give generous offering. Forgetting the warning of Laxman Sita came out beyond the lines of safety and was stolen away by Ravan.

In Jewelers' Block Insurance a vital Warranty is incorporated that after business hours all the jewelry be removed from Display Counter and be kept in the strong room chest along with cash from the cash counter. More often than not the Insured does not read this warranty. Many dacoit claims come intimating that at midnight jewelry worth Crores were stolen from display counter. Such claims get repudiated because the intimation letter itself contain the cause of repudiation like Janak Nandini was responsible for her own tragedy by overstepping the forbidden lines drawn by Laxman.

Lord Rama, Boatman and Marine Underwriting

Ahalya, a princess of Puru dynasty and married to great sage Gautama was cursed by her husband to turn into a stone and was returned to her human form only after being brushed by the dust from Lord Rama's feet. While wanting to cross the Ganges, the intuitive boatman refused to ferry Ramachandra across the river politely saying 'I have heard that with the touch of dust from your feet a stone had become a woman. While ferrying you, if my boat gets transformed into a woman by the dust touch of your feet my family will be ruined because this boat is the only means of earning my livelihood. Without my washing your feet with water and seeing them clean of dust, it will be risky on my part to get you into my boat. The legendary boatman was allowed by Lord Rama to do so. This rustic boatman was perhaps the first marine underwriter with adequate general awareness and the first pre-inspection surveyor in the history of Insurance. Fifty years ago a surveyor from Mumbai was deputed to Singapore to supervise the loading of palm oil into two ships. From a distance he casually looked at the activities of loading and gave a positive report. In fact the two ships were getting loaded with not palm oil but with water in containers and were scuttled during their voyage to Mumbai giving rise to fake claims still in their cognitive process of reaching judgment in the court.

Valmik Compensates and Sita Benefits

In the Valmik's Ashram Sita gave birth to Luv. It was the arrangement that when Sita would go the nearby rever for bath, she would leave back Luv in the custody of Ashram hermitess. One day Sita took her son alongwith her to the bathing ghat without informing the Ashramites. Valmik who was out suddenly arrived and found Luv missing. He was at his wit's end and thought he must have taken away by a tiger and got killed. Sita on her return from the bathing ghat could not bear such tragedy and might collapse into sudden death.He immediately took a blade of sacred grass called Kush and created another Luv with genetically identical cell so that Sita would not know about the tragedy.After a while Sita returned with Luv and found the look alike of Luv.Since the cloning was done from Kush grass, the second child was named Kush, much to her delight. A case of modern Inventory Loss. (Source:Somdev,Katha Sarit Sagar)

Krishna and Claim Settlement

Rukmi the prince of Vidarbha was very close to Shisupala. He fixed his sister Rukmini's marrige with him. Rukmini was not in favour of this proposal at all. Instead she wanted to marry Krishna. She sent a message to Krishna to rescue her from the trouble and marry her. Krishna did that in the right moment and Shisupal started abusing him.

Oracle was that Shisupal would be killed by Krishna the moment he commits hundred sins. The day he started abusing Daurpadi was the 100th sin he committed. While seding his Shudarshan Chakra to kill Shisupal in a great hurry, Krishna got his index finger cut accidentally and it started bleeding profusely. Spontaneously a teary-eyed Daurpadi at once tore apart a little piece of cloth from her saree and wrapped Krishna's injured finger to stop bleeding. Unknowingly the service she rendered to Krishna was the premium paid for protection against unforeseen circumstances. When Duryadhan in a disrespectful manner took away her saree one after another Krishna instantly replaced them one after another. It was the fastest claim settled with utmost dignity in the history of mankind. Krishna Himself was present at the claim site invisibly though.

The existence has given each one of us full potentiality to function through three channels: Channel of animality, Channel of humanity and the channel of divinity. It is all in our hands through which channel we want to respond and rise to the occasion.

CHAPTER 22

What is Ailing PSU Companies

At the time of Nationalisation in 1971, it was suggested to the then Government for making one Corporation like L.I.C .It was a prudently thought out proposal and had it been accepted, it could have prevented the present day disaster. Instead, four Companies were created. In the process these companies spent all their energy in fiercely competing among themselves and finally landed up in today's downfall.

Claim Hub: an Invitation to Disaster

In 2008 by introducing Claim Hubs as per the directives of the consultants, it brought an end to the age old practice of BMs and DMs settling claims of their clients which had kept cementing the good customer relationship. Every insurance policy is a promise given to the customer to be fulfilled in future in case of an accidental loss. With the centralised Claim Hub , promises are made by the marketing officials and claims are settled elsewhere by the strangers thus providing not services but inconveniences the clients.. It is embarrassing for marketing officials to approach such clients for renewal every year, in the process business is lost. Moreover in the whole process neither claim minimisation is intended nor becomes anybody's responsibility. The sense of belongingness and accountability too are diluted and lost. Our forefathers were neither fools nor are the private companies where the underwriter is invested with claim settlement responsibilies.

Brokers and Ruthless competition

Abolition of tariff and licensing of brokers have greatly reduced risk based market premium . The duty of an authentic broker is to arrange for the most appropriate cover at an appropriate rate. But in reality he gives the widest cover at the lowest possible rate by arranging competitive quotation from various companies which breaks the backbone of the Non-life insurance industry. Since this inappropriateness does not hamper his brokerage income, and insurance companies especially the PSUs are interested in growth and not profitability, this un-ethical practice has a firm footing in underwriting despite its ruinous consequences. Such aberrations were less prevalent among the agents.

Profaned Promotion Process

During recent decades, the Interview system in the promotions process from DGM to GM and CM to DGM cadres have been marred by more competent seniors being superseded by very low ranking and less efficient petty juniors due to favouritism. It was very painful humiliation for those who were superseded which demoralised the entire officers community and robbed off their enthusiasm to work .Those unscrupulous CEOs responsible, should know that for our organisation this sort of manipulation is as disastrous as making holes in the sailing ship. Such profanation was ubiquitous and dominated the promotion process of other cadres . For example one officer superseded 68 of his seniors to get his undeserving promotion. Imagine the collective agony, loss of enthusiasm and acute mental pain of those 68 superseded officers and its negative impact on the Company's productivity and its working atmosphere it must have.

The CEO of the Company is expected to be a man of

Character which means putting right man in right place. Large scale deviation of this godly principle has been one foremost reason which has caused these companies to sink to all time low. An organisation is not run as per the Management books but by the mindset of its leader and with such mean mentality of the CEOs no organisation can survive.

Hire Character; Train skills

The ancient Chinese built the Great Wall of China to live in peace and prosperity.   During the first hundred year of its existence,China was invaded three times,every time the hordes of enemy infantry had no need of climbing over the wall because they bribed the people at the gate and came through the doors.
They built the walls but forgot the character building of the people in charge of the security of the walls.They realized at last that the best defence against the enemy is not merely a fortified wall but the fortified character of its people. The quality of being honest is the surest way to prevent a personal mistake from contributing to the ultimate failure of the whole organization.

Medi-Claims and Inflated Hospital Bills

The moment the TPA gets involved , Insurance companies become vulnerable to the hospitals.

For example Mr.Ratnakar without insurance had his cataract operation done and paid Rs.16,000/-. His brother-in-law had the cataract operation from the same hospital by the same Doctor and estimate too was Rs.16000/-. Before payment ,his son informed that he had Health Insurance. The moment TPA got in touch with the Hospital ,the bill got increased and Rs.31,000 was paid as cashless settlement. Take the case of a cancer patient: For first surgery in April 23, the cashless settlement by the TPA , was for Rs.3,77,434/ .Similar amount was paid for the second surgery. During his third Surgery in July, 23 neither TPA nor the hospital was informed about insurance because there was no balance left in the Sum Insured. The bill came down from Rs 3,77, 434/- to Rs.180000/.

It is reported that a patient approached a certain hospital for an estimate and the estimate was for Rs.50,000/. After getting admitted he revealed that he had Medi-claim. After his treatment the bill came to Rs.2 lakh.He was told that the insurance Company paid only Rs.1.5 lakh and the rest amount of Rs.50,000/ was to be paid by him.

Such inflated bills are shockingly brutal for the Insurance Companies. Unknowingly the TPAs have become Achilles heel for Insurance Companies to be vulnerable in Mediclaim settlement. It is believed and feared that the Insured patients sometimes are unethically given overdose of medicines and are required to overstay in the hospital which are neither relevant to the treatment nor good for their health. It adversely affects the financial health of the insurance industry which ultimately sets off domino effects on the insured public in the form of abnormal increase in premium.

PSU companies seeking the helping hands from TPAs for settling claims reminds me of an ancient story. Pleased with the dedication of a village wood-cutter in the jungle ,one day God appeared before him and told him to express his wish for a boon and it will be fulfilled.The wood-cutter requested God to permit him a day's time to consult his wife and the elders in the village.God said be it so and disappeared.The elders in the village advised him to ask for gold so that he would be rich and live happily.But his wife said gold could be stolen.It would be better to ask for two more hands so that he would cut more wood and more earning will make the family happy. He followed his wife's advice and God gave him two more hands.With four hands he immediately felt uncomfortable.His first two hands lost strength and became inoperative. He did not know how to get things done from additional hands which became burden on him.In the process he lost his movement and finally became ruined.

Insurace Companies inviting TPA to do their job is like inviting trouble. Companies like Bajaj Allianz and Star Health usually do not utilize TPA but perform better by utilizing their own manpower who work with sense of belongingness and not forgetting the interest of their respective companies which is of prime importance in any business transaction.One cannot expect this from a TPA.

The better alternative is to give 10 % discount in premium to the Insured opting for reimbursement claims alongwith 10 % further discount for 10% Co-Pay.It may prevent more than 30% leakages.Otherwise PSUs will fail to prevent privatization.

Team visit to the Claim Site

A huge stock of wheat, insured by a private Company, was affected by flood in Haryana. On receiving intimation of loss for Rs.73 Cr. officials from their Delhi Office visited the site with a surveyor. Affected stock was segregated. Related documents were obtained and the claim was assessed for Rs.3 Cr. and was paid within weeks which amounts to only 4% of the total estimate.

Few years back there was a huge fire in Byculla, Mumbai. The concerned private insurance company was informed that the estimate of loss would be about Rs.50 Crore. Within hours the Company's Claim head, Marketing Head and Head of the Risk management along with a surveyor were at the site. After their physical inspection, instantly the estimate came down to Rs.10 lakh which was only 2% of the initial estimate.

It may sound strange but true.It is but natural that the loss looks much bigger at the time of the event taking place. Had it been a PSU claim, the assessment would have been otherwise because of non-visit of Claim management team from PSU companies. It is very unfortunate. They should follow the private sector method of immediate visit to the site and keep monitoring the assessment before the survey report is released if they are really interested in prudent claims management.

In the absence of team visit such leakages are normal happenings, maybe in varying degrees. In one Conference the Chairman of a PSU Company said "Leakages in claims are to the tune of 20%". But he did not take any step to prevent it.

Training Centres impart only information. Visiting the accident site is the only way for the Insurance Officials to learn tricks of the trade because such practical experiences stimulate their love for the profession and make their intelligence start functioning . With such participation they will be full of insight, their vision will be unclouded, and in their very presence the right will happen of its own accord. Since they do not visit, their Company suffers and they do not grow up.

During this age of cut throat competition, Private companies like ICICI Lombard and Bajaj Allianz make profit not for underwriting skills but due to their effective claims management system in place.

Chapter 23

Application of Intelligence in Claims

There are three kinds of intelligence. Intelligence of the body which is called instinct .Body is the hardware and instinct is the software. Second one is intellect whose hardware is brain. Third one is intuition whose hardware is heart.It is only when someone deeply loves his job, his heart responds and intuition starts functioning. Let us analyse two real life examples below:

The benefit of Insatiable Curiosity

BHEL,the giant PSU heavy electrical machinery manufacturer, had covered its transformer generator erection project for Maharastra Electricity Board under Erection All Risk policy . The transformer burst violently due to sudden surge and the loss was claimed as a Constructive Total Loss. Competent Authority appointed a surveyor and after inspection and documentation he assessed the loss as CTL , the cost of repair being as much as the cost of replacement. BHEL agreed and the salvage which constituted of valuable copper was to be surrendered to insurer as per procedure. The surveyor was entrusted with the process of calling quotes from the market and recommending to the insurers to accept and award to the highest bidder. The same was received by United India office and the underwriters found that the salvage value was as much as 35 per cent of our total liability of Rs 4 crore. All their claims committee members were very happy that such a substantial salvege proceeds reduced our liability by almost Rs1.10 crore. But the Head of the office had insatiable curiosity of a genius and exceptional originality to think out of box in case of major claims and before taking the decision his intuitive mind led him to visit a site in internet to see the current market value of high quality bulk copper used in generator transformers and was pleasantly surprised that the same has appreciated by 300% during last 1 year which translated into a salvage value of the scrap at Rs 4.15 crore . He calculated the value of copper salvage by multiplying the weight with the present market price. He again cross checked with a friend who was aware of the material prices and he came back to him telling that he was right. He phoned of the surveyor and wanted to confirm whether we should go ahead with his calculation and he emphatically said YES.

The prudent Officer visited BHEL and met GM ,Materials, and asked him about the last price of salvage sold. The GM told ,as per rule, they did that through another PSU Metal Scrap Corporation and the last auction was 2 years back. The Officer asked him whether he was aware of the current value of copper scrap and he said that he was not. The GM asked me as to why he was seeking this information. He told him,' Sir I wish to give you a very exciting news ,"You are sitting over a pile of gold because your copper price has appreciated by 300 per cent in last 1 year." He told him he was going to generate a profit by paying the transformer claim from the sale of salvage. GM of BHEL phoned up certain sources to ascertain what theUI officer was telling and he was convinced it as true. He called the GM, Projects and they had a long and valuable discussion on the subject They profusely thanked the Insurance Official for opening their eyes . After a fortnight ,BHEL wrote to UI that they would not pursue the claim any more. UI office took a legally binding letter and closed the claim with HO's approval. UI office requested their HO not to appoint this surveyor henceforth for obvious reasons.

Thus two birds were killed in one stone. UI's liability was nil and BHEL woke up to the pleasant reality. It was a win-win situation for both t. All is well that ends well.

Lesson learnt : Experts need not be blindly trusted, high degree of belongingness for the organisation and application of intution are essential for the officials given power and responsibility.

Weathering the Weather Insurance Claims

Jaisalmer is a former medieval trading centre and a princely state in Rajasthan,in the heart of the Thar desert. A claim for Rs.7 crore from that taluka was put up for approval because on a particular day it rained heavily and the weather station recorded 96 mm heavy rainfall. Many farmers suffered losses and accordingly their claims were made. But in a desert like Thar if it had rained so much it would have been a world news. There was no news paper reporting no government's weather department record ; it was only on the basis of a a certificate from a Private weather station of that area , such a huge claim was raised.

Since there was no other confirmation on such unusual heavy rainfall and Sum Insured of the individual farmers were abnormally large, it was decided that weather station report of the day has to be verified before any further investigation. When the report arrived in the Insurance office, to the shock and surprise of the officials concerned figure of rainfall recorded was 0.96 mm which was less than 01 mm and was wrongly read and perceived as 96mm. In a public sector everyone thinks that the other must have read the file. In the process sometimes nobody reads before signing and the claim gets processed.

The officers who recommended the claim for approval were very casual in their approach. They submitted the file without reading it. They did not love their job. Their general awareness was poor. Jaisalmer area was in the heart of Thar desert. Such huge rainfall is almost impossible in a single day. They should have applied their common sense to have it investigated. Such examples are not exceptions in big claims, the details of which cannot not be discussed in print. In such cases a quick visit to the claim site by the Claim management team is a favored option.

The Persuasive Skill

A   carelessly fast with breakneck speed Mahindra Bolero performed an acrobatic movement in the air and turned upside down after a side ward somersault when the driver applied sudden break to avoid collision with a road crossing buffalo.The insured who was travelling with his whole family. Although the strongly built car was considerably damaged, the insured and all his family members escaped unhurt. The surveyor assessed the loss on the behalf of the insurance company and recommended that body of the car is reparable. The Insured a Saradar asked for replacement of the whole body saying that it is inauspicious to retain the same body after such unfortunate mishap. The surveyor politely responded saying, 'Sir,you should rather be grateful to the body of the car who saved the life of your entire family by hurling itself on the ground as a protective armor. It is your real Saviour.' The insured, a tough Saradar was speechless, re–collected the horror of the accident with closed eyes, expressed his gratitude in tears and nodded his head indicating affirmative response. All is well that ends well.

Chapter 24

Business Inturruption Claims:a Challenge for the PSU

Veni, vidi,vici' I came, I saw,I conquered, uttered Julius Caesar after conquering Asia Minor (present day Turkey) in a bit stylish bragging that had impressed many of the writers of his day and beyod.If we visit the site of claim,we shall not only see and feel the truth but the doubt about the occurrence of the event will be removed forever.

A Business Interruption Policy was issued to a plastic manufacturing industry with supplier's end extension to Gas supplying Company. A claim was reported that cooling tower had collapsed as a result of which there had been short supply of 3900 MT of gas every day to the Insured's plastic industry.

A surveyor, who was an engineer, was appointed to

assess B.I claim. Nobody bothered to know about the survey of the 25 year old Cooling Tower for material damage claim since it is an important condition of the BI policdy that BI claim is payable only if the material damage Claim is admissible. Neither a surveyor was deputed nor any official team visited to the supplier's site to ascertain the auntheicity of the accident. Sad.

Finally Survey Report came witn an assessment of Rs.162 Cr. Briefly the details are as follows: Loss of Gross Profit per day Rs.80 lakh for 120 days (indemnity period and the time took for repair of the cooling tower)= Rs.96 Cr. The insured had made extra efforts to reduce shortage in Turnover and thus submitted a bill for Rs36 Cr. towards Increased Cost of Working for reducing the shortage in Gross Profit by Rs.30 Cr. Since maximum amount of ICW payable cannot be more than reduction in the shortage of GP, in this case Rs.30 Cr.was the maximum liability of the Insurer to reimburse.Therefore the total amount of Claim was (Rs.96.Cr + Rs.30) =Rs.126 Cr. Again since the loss of gross profit had been calculated as constant from the first day till the last day@ Rs.80 Cr.per day, there had been no contribution of ICW. Hence even Rs.30 Cr. not payable either.The learned surveyor instead of adding lower of the two, added both the items to the Claim amount and submitted his report with assessed amount for Rs.162Cr.(Rs.96Cr.+Rs.36 Cr.+ Rs30 Cr) instead of (Rs.96 Cr.only)

Hence Rs.30 Cr.was paid twice and Rs.36 Cr.was wrongly paid out of utter ignorance of the Surveyor and stupidity of the learned insurance officials.The latter could have got the assessment checked by a competent C.A by which the underwriters would have saved Rs.66 Cr towards leakages in the first instance.

Nobody in the Claims processing team right from the bottom to the top had the interest and insight to read and analyze the assessment. Nobody bothered to know whether the supplier had lodged a material damage claim or not under his policy which is basis that decides the liability of the BI claim. This speaks volumes about the idle and lackadaisical manner in which such huge amount of sensitive claims are handled in the PSU companies. And you must now guess what must have happened to this particular claim. The Survoyer did not know the basic principles of BI. The officer who appointed him had no interest in his Company's interest. The officers in the claims at Regional and Head Office were annoyingly lacking in will and enthusiasm. With such kind of leakages how does one expect that PSU companies will make underwriting profit.

Another such Claim with another Surveyor

That year in December six months after the first claim another 25 year old cooling tower was reported to have been shut down for maintenance from the same Insured under the same policy . Forty five days after this intimation was received another surveyor was appointed for BI claim. The short supply of gas per day was more or less the same quantity of about 3900 MT.The learned surveyor assessed the loss of Gross Profit @ Rs.50 lakh per day (as against Rs.80 lakh per day assessed by the previous surveyor) .The duration of repair was 100 days. Hence he arrived at Rs 50 crore as the final assessment.

Short supply of Gas per day remaining of the same quantity, shortage of gross profit of Rs.80 lakh per day in previous claim is a mind-blowing experience. Both the claims in all respects were not similar but arithmetically the same.But first claim was assessed at Rs.162 Cr. where as the second one was assessed for Rs.50 Cr. It is because the surveyor was different despite the insurance officials were being the same. The excess of Rs. 30 lakh shortage of GP per day in the first claim is no way acceptable because both the surveyors relied on the same documentations. In short more than Rs.100 Cr. of excess amount was paid in the first claim which could have been prevented if the claim would have been handled with with wisdom and sincerity.About the second claim less said the better.

Lessons Learnt

History repeats itself . Man does not learn from its repetition. Experts say that in of case of BI claims appointing a Chartered Accountant Surveyor is essential because he is qualified and competent to analyse the reports and statements submitted by the Insured's Cost auditors,Statutary auditors,GST auditors with Unique Document Identification Number to assess the loss and recommend indemnification. There is no reason why Engineers should be appointed for such claims.The surveyor must give report on the authenticity of the Material damage Claim if not assessment. For Insurance officials, true learning happens at Claim Sites and not in the class rooms at Training Centres.In the above two cases if a team of officials would have visited both the sites on both the occasions along with the surveyors, they could have checked the following:The cause of accident since both the Cooling Towers were 25 years old. When the repair started and when completed.The type of Claim lodged with the Insurance Company which had insured the cooling Towers. Material damage Liability admitted or not by the said insurance Company. Modus Operandi of ICW: from which other source gas was obtained and details of payment to the interim supplier. There were too many serious anomalies in both the claims which could have been looked into at the time of assessment. All that cannot be discussed in print.

By reading books on Driving, one cannot drive a vehicle.Reading books on swimming one cannot learn swimming.Reading survey reports one cannot become an effective claims manager.Visiting the site will give us the experience of true learning. In this world nothing can be taught, everything can be learnt.Claim Sites, and not class rooms are our true learning Centres provided we have love for the job we are doing.

The people who handled these two claims might have been Engineers, professionals with Fellowship and MBAs with decades of experience .But what are these qualifications worth , if we do not have practical experience and do not use our intelligence, if we do not have the religious zeal that drives us to know the truth for which we are paid by the Commpany.There is no other way to learn deeper than visiting the site of Claim and participating in claim assessment.This will help us to grow in wisdom and expand in awareness in life. And that is how our Company will grow with our growing.

■

Black Eagle Books

www.blackeaglebooks.org
info@blackeaglebooks.org

Black Eagle Books, an independent publisher, was founded as a nonprofit organization in April, 2019. It is our mission to connect and engage the Indian diaspora and the world at large with the best of works of world literature published on a collaborative platform, with special emphasis on foregrounding Contemporary Classics and New Writing.

www.ingramcontent.com/pod-product-compliance
Lightning Source LLC
Chambersburg PA
CBHW030455210326
41597CB00013B/684